Peter Voice

Illustrations by Christian Gastaldello

A Bit of **French** With Your **Coffee** and **Croissants**

novum ✺ pro

This book is also available as e-book.

www.novum-publishing.co.uk

© 2022 novum publishing

ISBN 978-3-99131-275-8
Editing: Hugo Chandler, BA;
Kathleen Moreira
Cover photos:
Khotcharak Siriwong, Nearbirds,
Alexandra Smirnova | Dreamstime.com
Cover design, layout & typesetting:
novum publishing
Internal illustrations:
Christian Gastaldello

The images provided by the author have been printed in the highest possible quality.

www.novum-publishing.co.uk

Climate neutral
Print product
ClimatePartner.com/16547-2201-1002

La Tour Eiffel

Le Louvre

*To my mum and dad for finding the money
to send me on a school trip to Paris in 1966;
To my French teacher, Mrs Andrews,
who organised and led us on that trip; and
who subsequently arranged for me to stay with a French family;
To that French family in Brive and Argentat
for their life-long kindness and friendship; and
To Casterbridge Tours for enabling me to continue to travel
and to learn, like our customers, for so many years.*

Le Lycée St. Louis, Boulevard St. Michel

Foreword

The prolonged period of lockdown has given me the time to write this book. It is intended as a coffee-table book; one that hopefully you might spill your coffee over, and thus spare yourself the prospect of tackling the section on French grammar and, indeed, the extensive lists of expressions and vocabulary in the appendices. The illustrations are by the artist, Christian Gastaldello, a good friend of mine, and fellow French explorer and Francophile. This is a book of French words interspersed with anecdotes. I take full responsibility for any mistakes you may discover. Please correct them yourself using a red-ink pen. Part 8 is devoted to George Voice, the oldest brother of my father, who was killed during the First World War at the age of 22. He is buried in the British Cemetery at Honnechy in Northern France. What is most important, as you probably realise, is that you purchase and possess your personal copy of this book.

Le Parking, Arromanches

Bilateral exchanges

France is a beautiful country. There is no dispute. England, and the rest of the UK, is just as beautiful. The French speak French. The English speak English. A lot of French and English people learn to speak each other's language.

En voici deux exemples:

One summer, I was standing outside the 6 June 1944 D-Day Museum in Arromanches. It was a glorious day. There is a large *parking* in front of the museum. An attractive woman was trying to extract a ticket from the machine. She tried several times. Finally, she turned around and saw an official looking man. In a raised (not unpleasant) voice, she called to him in her best French:

"Monsieur! Est-ce que vous trraav eye yeh eeci?"

To which, after a moment's hesitation, he replied:

"Madame, je porte cet uniforme tous les jours pour le plaisir. Comment puis-je vous aider? Ow may I elp you?"

She went weak at the knees. He took her coins, placed them in the slot, pressed a button and extracted a ticket. He escorted her back to her car, her husband and three kids, and wished her:

"Bonne continuation de la journée, Madame".

The granddaughter of the French family with whom I first stayed as a schoolboy, once asked me the following question in her best English:

"Do you ave a *petatom*?"

"A *petatom*?" I replied inquisitively.

I repeated the question to myself out loud.

"Do I have a *petatom*?" *A petatom* sounded like a word just shot from a machine gun at point blank range.

What she had asked me was: "Do you have A – Pet – At – Home?" Stéphanie, the girl in question, is now a fully trained, practising vet and also has a husband, three children and several pets of her own. She could have asked me simply: "Do you have a dog or a cat?" But I suppose she did not want to exclude the possibility that I might have a goldfish (*un poisson rouge*), a mouse (*une souris*), a guinea pig (*un cochon d'Inde*), a hamster *(un hamster)*, a gerbil (*une gerbille*), a ferret (*un furet*), a rabbit (*un lapin*) or perhaps a snake (*un serpent*).

In my home town there is actually a pet store called Pets at Home which I call *Petsatom*.

A pet is *un animal de compagnie* – literally a companion animal – which leads me to think that Stéphanie could have asked me: "Do you have a company animal?" In which case, I might have had visions of the company donkey being present at the Annual General Meeting. Strictly speaking, in veterinary parlance, a donkey (*un âne*) would be *un animal domestique* like a horse (*un cheval*), a cow (*une vache*), a sheep (*un mouton*) and a goat (*une chèvre*); as opposed to *un animal sauvage,* like *un écureuil* (squirrel), *un blaireau* (badger), *une loutre* (otter), *un renard* (fox), *un castor* (beaver), *un singe* (monkey), *un gorille, une girafe, un tigre, un lion, un éléphant* and *un guépard* (a cheetah) etc. See Appendix 5 for some French expressions with animals.

Could all those in favour say "Eee-aw"

Part 1

L'Entente Cordiale

Exchange of Words Between Neighbours

*L'Entrée au Hameau de Marie Antoinette
dans le Parc de Versailles*

Les Anglais

When in France, my ears prick up if I should overhear someone speak about *les Anglais, les Anglaises, les Anglo-Saxons, les Britanniques, l'Angleterre, la Grande-Bretagne* or *le Royaume-Uni.*

Victor Hugo once said, "There is no animosity between our two nations; only a desire to surpass."

If things are not going well or life is tough, as long as the French can point to a more unfavourable situation in England, then they can somehow reassure themselves that things could be a lot worse.

Paris will host the XXXIII Jeux Olympiques (*les JO*) in 2024. I have no doubt that they will be even more successful than the London Olympic Games of 2012. The Opening Ceremony will be spectacular, featuring the resurrection of Johnny Hallyday, and the rejuvenation and cloning of Brigitte Bardot; the *pièce de la résistance* will be a celebrity 100 metres race in which Gérard Depardieu will be given a two minute head-start. The Olympic Flame will be lit by a woman called *Marianne*, draped in the *tricolore* and singing the *Marseillaise.*

The French national football team is currently superior, having won two recent FIFA World Cups; there is not much to choose between our men's or women's rugby teams; the French are, and will always be, French champions of *pétanque*; and at least one Frenchman (*Alain Robert*) has been trained to climb tall buildings with his bare hands and no ropes. I don't know of (m)any French players of cricket, darts or snooker. On food and drink, the French find it hard to believe that the English can make good quality wines and cheeses; they have *pâté de foie gras* and we have baked beans and marmite. On the economy, rising unemployment and inflation is manageable if it is thought to be rising faster in the UK, whether it is or it is not. And, of course, the French drive on the **right** side of the road. But so do we when we are in France.

Do not be alarmed if you should hear: *"Je vais manger un onglet."* The French are not cannibals. *Un onglet (*literally *a thimble) de boeuf* is a cut or *tranche de filet de boeuf* (of beef steak), as are *pavé, bavette, entrecôte, tournedos* and *chateaubriand/châteaubriant*. You can simply order *un bifteck* or *un steak (et) frites*. Usually, *comme la plupart des Anglais*, you will be expected to ask for *la cuisson* to be *(bien) bien cuit*, unless you prefer it less well-done, then it is *à point;* or *saignant* or *bleu*, almost uncooked, in which case you might also like *le steak tartare / filet américain*.

You might hear someone say: *"il fait un temps comme en Angleterre"*, when it is pouring with rain, or the weather is just miserable. As opposed perhaps to: *"il pleut des hallebardes", "il pleut des cordes"* or *"il fait un après-midi de chien"*. See Appendix 4 for some weather vocabulary.

Une assiette anglaise is a plate of assorted cold meats. *La crème anglaise* is custard. *Une clé anglaise* is a monkey wrench or adjustable spanner. *Les cannes anglaises* are crutches!

But worse are: *"les Anglais sont débarqués"* when for women it's that time of the month/*les règles*; and *filer à l'anglaise* which is to leave without permission or without paying, usually at speed and without warning.

And, not least, with *le Brexit, le variant anglais* (of the *coronavirus*) and the initial problems with the supply of vaccines, our French friends have more ammunition than ever to accuse us of being traitors from *la perfide Albion*. *"Que Dieu sauve la reine!"*

Well, of course, we, *les Anglais*, can play French cricket, take French leave, and when we let slip a swear word (*"Zut alors!"* was all I was taught at school) we can say: *"Excuse my French!"* *Les Français*, those annoying French people, don't you just love them and *la belle France*, if not necessarily both, and in that order.

Du Franglais

La langue française is enriched with many English words; and the French do have a tendency, especially in the media, to use English words where there is a perfectly good French alternative. The world of computers, phones, business, science and sport are a rich source of English vocabulary, a lot of which emanates from America. There was a time when the French government and *les immortels* of the *Académie française*[1] tried to defend the French language from such an invasion. Laws were even passed. Such tensions seem to have eased. And, in case you were wondering, *hélas, eh bien oui, les immortels* do not live forever but they do get constantly replenished.

Some words are not used as in English and their meaning is not always clear:

Le baby-foot is table football; *les flippers* are pin ball machines; *le ball-trap* is clay-pigeon shooting; *les peoples* are celebrities; *le lifting* is a face-lift; *le relooking* is a make-over; *le brushing* is a blow-dry; *le string* is a thong and *un smoking* is a dinner jacket; *un short* is a pair of shorts; *le pressing* is the dry-cleaners or dry cleaning. *Le zapping* and the verb *zapper* mean to switch TV channels.

Le slam is live performance poetry. *Les seniors* are older people.

Other such words could not be clearer: *le week-end, un sandwich, un coca cola* (*un coca cola light* is a diet coke), *du ketchup, les squatteurs,*

---

1 The Académie française was founded in 1635 by Cardinal Richelieu with 40 members (immortels). Its aim is to observe, monitor and develop the French language; and to contain its excesses, by producing and updating grammar rules and a dictionary. In 1990, it produced a recommendation to simplify spelling of over 2,000 words; this reform has been incorporated into French school text books since 2016. As the Académie acknowledges, the recommended simplifications will be accepted only through usage over time; and, therefore, both the old and new spellings will be accepted as correct. See references in Part 5 and the bibliography.

un parking (a car park or parking slot), *le bulldozer, le ferry-boat, le bungalow, un camping* (a camp site), *un milkshake, un smoothie, le tennis, le football, le rugby, le chewing-gum…*

I think *le fair-play anglais* may be a little less used at the moment. In the current climate of coronavirus and lockdown, you may hear reference to "*des clusters*" of new positive Covid cases; and to "*le click and collect*" for purchases made on-line for collection at a nearby shop.

Some Franglish

We do, of course, entertain as many French words as possible in the English language. They are not so frequently used; and, when we do use them, it is often tongue-in-cheek or in a light-hearted manner. Sometimes, *le mot juste* just happens to be a French one: *Femme fatale, bête noire, pièce de résistance, coup de grâce, fait accompli, faux pas, pied-à-terre, déjà vu, étiquette, rendez-vous, boudoir, tour de force, vernissage, entourage, boutique, concierge, agent provocateur, crime passionnel;*
Cuisine, cordon-bleu, chef, gâteau, soufflé, bon appétit;
"Voilà! Oh là là! Très chic! Bon voyage! C'est la vie! N'est-ce pas?"
can all be used when needing to add a touch of humour!
"Mange-tout Rodney, *mange-tout!"* (David Jason in Only Fools and Horses).

My mother told me that she once went to M&S to buy a skirt and the inside label (*une étiquette*) had "*tour de hanches*" (hip size) printed on it. She immediately put it back on the rail, declaring: "I am not wearing anything labelled tour de haunches!"
A German girl told me that she did not like the English kitchen; I realised she meant English *cuisine*. I told her that I liked bratwurst and sauerkraut. That was as far as it went.
"N'est-ce pas?" is very versatile, "*n'est-ce pas?*" It can be tagged on to any French and indeed any English sentence. However, its literal English translation will vary depending on the sentence it is attached to: *"The English play cricket, **isn't it**?"*
*"You lost, **isn't it**?". "You have done it, **isn't it**?".* (**don't they**? **didn't you**? **have n't you**?), "*n'est-ce pas?*"

Fractured French

Some French expressions lend themselves to humorous mis-translations based on an English mis-pronunciation. An American F. S. Pearson published, as far back as 1950, an illustrated compilation of such examples in his book "Fractured French".

Some examples:
Un apéritif: a set of dentures.
Le coup de grâce: a lawn mower.
La pièce de résistance: a young woman resisting the charms of her suitors.
Châteauneuf-du-Pape: My father comes from Newcastle.
Le sang-froid anglais: an Englishman with a bloody cold.
Merci! Merci!: Take pity on me!
S'il vous plaît: silver plate.
Pas de deux: a father of twins.
Tête-à-tête: a closely-fitting bra.
Tout de suite: too much sugar in my tea.
L'Entente Cordiale: In the Drinks Tent.
Correspondance: a place for writing letters in the Paris *Métro*.
Moi aussi: I'm Australian.

Fractured English

The French could try something similar:
No Smoking: *Tenue de soirée, pas de rigueur.*
Free House: *Habitation sans loyer.*
Free cash withdrawals: *Les Anglais sont généreux.*

Heavy Plant Crossing: *Les arbres anglais se déplacent.*

No Fly Tipping: *Pas de mouches ici.*
Car Boot Sale: *Vente de bottes de voiture.*

Greetings

The French do a lot of hand-shaking (*serrer la main à qqn.*) and kissing on cheeks (*faire la bise à qqn.*) when they meet and greet each other. The English are much more reserved. When in France do as the French do. By that, I don't mean greet people you hardly know by attempting to kiss them on the cheeks as many times as you can. But respond in kind to any friendly gestures made. Shaking hands is acceptable, more frequent, and much less formal than in England.

During the coronavirus *pandémie*, it has been necessary to respect *les gestes barrières*, including *la distanciation sociale d'un mètre,* which therefore excludes cheek kissing and shaking hands. So, relax: "*Décontractez-vous!*"; or: "*Gardez le sang-froid anglais*", meaning: "Stay cool"; and not: "Keep away from that Englishman with the bloody cold".

Enchanté (*enchantée* if you are female) -pleased to meet you- is probably the quickest chat-up line. That still doesn't give you the *feu vert* to plant kisses (*bisous/bises*) on cheeks (*joues*). As for the follow up, you will just have to play it by ear. For extricating yourself if the *dénouement* should *tourner mal,* see a selection of swear words in Appendix 13 [for example, "*À bas les mains, connard!*"]

When you enter a shop, a restaurant, a café or a lift, it is polite to say "*Bonjour*", and preferably "*Bonjour Monsieur*", "*Bonjour Madame*" or "*Bonjour Mademoiselle*". If there is one of each gender, then you can say "*Bonjour Monsieur, Dame*" or, if several, then "*Bonjour Messieurs, Dames*". And on leaving you can say "*Au revoir, Monsieur*" *etc.*, unless you've decided to *filer à l'anglaise*, in which case just turn and run when you think the coast is clear. These rules do not apply should you be brave enough to enter public toilets. Except, of course, if you should happen on *une dame pipi*, sitting at a table doing some knitting or reading a book; and collecting at least 50 centimes for keeping the place clean and directing you to the next available *pissoir* or *cabine*. A simple "*Merci Madame*" should suffice on leaving, unless you haven't paid, in which case all hell will likely let loose (*Madame va se mettre à gueuler*).

Of course, you can also wish someone *"Bonne journée"* (have a nice day) or *"Bonne soirée"* (have a good evening). You might hear someone say: *"Bonne continuation de l'après-midi"*. A suitable reply might be *"Merci, à vous aussi"*.

In the evening, you can say *"Bonsoir"*, both for good evening and goodbye/goodnight. *"Bonne nuit"* is usually reserved for just before bedtime.

"Au revoir" is goodbye; and *"Adieu"* really is goodbye or farewell; *"Salut!"* is the informal hi! and bye!; and some French people will say *"Bye Bye!"* *"À bientôt"* is See you soon, *"À tout à l'heure"*: See you later, *"À tantôt"*: See you later on, and *"À tout de suite"*: See you very shortly.

Some things are more palatable or sound better in French?

Le papier hygiénique: toilet paper.

Faire sa toilette: to get washed and dressed.

Les escargots: snails.

Les éoliennes: wind turbines.

Le bras d'honneur: the French equivalent of the "V" sign.

Vous êtes invités à ne pas marcher sur la pelouse: Keep off the grass.

Les déjections canines = les crottes de chien.

Dégustation de vins: wine tasting.

L'ostréiculture/la mytiliculture/l'héliciculture: oyster farming/mussel farming/snail farming.

Une trottinette électrique: an electric scooter.

Une moissoneuse-batteuse: a combine-harvester.

Un paradis fiscal: a tax haven.

La bio: organic farming, food or production (*l'agriculture biologique, les produits bio, l'alimentation bio*)

M'as-tu vue ?

J'aime ma trottinette électrique

Un(e) m'as-tu-vu(e): a show off; a poser; an attention seeker.

Un pamplemousse: a grapefruit.

Le Bureau de Perception: the Tax Office.

Le temps des cerises: the good times in the past (cherry blossom/ picking time).

Le pantouflage: highly trained civil servants/ ministers go off to work in the private sector.

Faire du piston/se faire pistonner: to make use of friends in high places to advance in your career or life.

La lanterne rouge: the wooden spoon (awarded to the person or team in last place).

Un pot-de-vin: a bribe.

Aux frais de la princesse: on the house; free of charge; scot-free.

Faire chanter qqn: to blackmail someone.

Du chantage: blackmail.

Les Franciliens: inhabitants of the region of Île-de- France (Paris region).

Un violon d'Ingres: a hobby (one which you could also do professionally).

French Alphabet

If you know how to pronounce the letters of the French alphabet, you can at least spell (*épeler*) your own name (*prénom, nom de famille*) and pronounce the abbreviations/acronyms (*les sigles*) on the next pages. Here is my own devised phonetic version.

Note F, L, M, N, O, S and Z are pronounced as in English.

Note French G is like the French *j'ai;* and French J is like szjee (with szj as in **Z**a Za Gabor or French *Jean* + ee));

French u is like trying to say oo preceded by ee (ee oo).

A a in cat	N N
B bay	O O
C say	P pay
D day	Q keeoo
E er/a É ay	R air
F F	S S
G j'ai	T tay
H ash	U eeoo
I ee	V vay
J jee (j as <u>Z</u>a Za Gabor)	W doobler vay
K car	X eeks
L L	Y ee greck
M M	Z Z (zed)

Some examples: Où est le WC (doobler vay/say)? (You can also just say **vay/say**).
VAR is vay/a/air!
RSVP: air/S/vay/pay.
ADN: a/day/N (=DNA).
Je m'appelle Boris: bay/O/air/ee/S.
Olivia: O/L/ee/vay/ee/a.
Phoebe: pay/ash/o/er/bay/er.
Zara: zed/a/air/a.
George: j'ai/er/O/air/j'ai/er.
Julian: jee/eeoo/L/ee/a/N.

Les Sigles (abbreviations/<u>acronyms</u>)

ADN	Acide désoxyribonucléique	DNA dioxyribonucle-ic acid
Les LBD	Lanceurs de balles de défense	Rubber bullet weapons
Le PSG	Paris St. Germain	PSG football club
Les <u>Ehpad</u>	Etablissements d'héberge-ment des personnes âgées et dépendantes	Care homes
L'IVG	Interruption volontaire de grossesse	Abortion
La TVA	Taxe à la valeur ajoutée	VAT
Le / La <u>VAR</u>	Video assistant referee	Also le Var is a French département
Les VTC	Voitures de tourisme avec chauffeur	French "Uber"
Les ASVP	Agents de surveillance de la voie publique	Community police/support officers
Le <u>SAMU</u>	Service d'aide médicale d'urgence	Ambulance and Paramedic Services
Les JO	Jeux Olympiques	Olympic Games
Les WC	Water Closet	WC; toilets

Un <u>OVNI</u>	Objet volant non-identifié	UFO (unidentified flying object)
Les OGM	Organismes génétiquement modifiés	GMO
La SNCF	Société des chemins de fer français	French Railways
La RATP	Régie autonome des transports parisiens	Paris Métro and bus services company
Le RER	Réseau express régional	Paris and suburbs fast train service
L'OMS	Organisation mondiale de la santé	WHO (World Health Organisation)
L'<u>OTAN</u>	Organisation du traité de l'Atlantique Nord	NATO
L'<u>ONU</u>	Organisation des nations unies	UNO
L'OMC	Organisation mondiale de commerce	WTO (World Trade Organisation)
La CEDH	Cour européenne des droits humains	ECHR
Les HLM	Habitations à loyer modéré	Low rent social housing
Les SDF/ les sans-abri	Sans domicile fixe	Homeless people
Le PMU	Pari mutuel urbain	French betting shop
L'IMC	Indice de masse corporel	BMI (Body mass index)
RSVP	Répondez s'il vous plaît	RSVP (Please reply)

La CRS	Compagnie républicaine de sécurité	Paramilitary police on motor bikes
La RN	Route nationale	Motorway M
La RF	République française	French Republic
Le VTT	Vélo tout terrain	Mountain bike
Les BD	Bandes dessinées	Comic strips/comics
Le SMIC	Salaire minimum interprofessionnel de croissance	Minimum wage
Les PME	Petites et moyennes entreprises	Small and medium sized firms
La VO	Version originale	Original version of film
La VF	Version française	French version of film
Le SIDA	Syndrome immunodéficitaire acquis	AIDS Auto-immune deficiency syndrome
L'ENA	École Nationale d'Administration	Top training school for civil servants
L'AOC	Appellation d'origine contrôlée	Protected origin status
L'UE	Union europénne	EU European Union
en PACA	en région Provence–Alpes–Côte d'Azur	In the Provence-Alpes-Côte d'Azur region
Le QR code	Le QR code	Quick Response code

Some commonly abbreviated words mostly in conversation:

Les accros	Les accrochés (addicts, fans)
Les ados	Les adolescents
La clim	La climatisation (air conditioning)
La voiture d'occas	La voiture d'occasion (second-hand car)
Le p'tit déj	Le petit déjeuner (breakfast)
La pub	La publicité (adverts)
Un appart	Un appartement
Une appli	Une application (an app)
Un apéro	Un apéritif
Une manif	Une manifestation (demonstration)
Le frigo	Le réfrigérateur (fridge)

Pronunciation of some French place names

Angers *(*last syllable like French *j'ai).*
Bay*eux (*first syllable like English *bye* + *yer).*
Caen *(*rhymes in French with *quand, camp, con).*
Le **Lot**-*et-Garonne/dans le* **Lot** *(*as in English word "lot"; and not "low" as in *le gros lot* the jackpot or *le lot de vaccins* the batch of vaccines).*
*Mi***llau** (like English me + yo).
Quimp*er (*like camp air in English*).*
Reims *(pronounced reams in English; but rance (as in rancid) in French).*

Les villes jumelées (twinned towns)

In a special edition of The Punch Magazine in 1976, entitled "What French Connection?", Miles Kington suggested that the twinning of English and French towns could do with a boost. He thought, for example, it would be a good idea to twin Ware with Caen (which rhymes with *quand/*when):
"The French have always been fond of abstract philosophic questions, such as Ow? and Vot? Here is the ideal opportunity to enshrine two more:
Ware (où?) and Caen (ven?). Vere and ven did you last see your father? Vere and ven shall we zree meet again? Just two of the many problems to be thrashed out by the Ware–Caen Debating Society".
In this spirit, I would like to evoke the little known twinning of Casterbridge in Wessex with Balbec in Normandy. The mayor of the former, with the assistance of Casterbridge Tours of Sherborne, Dorset, was able to arrange for young Thomas Hardy to visit the Proust family and their son Marcel. All went well until Tom lost his anachronistic wrist-watch. He and Marcel subsequently spent several days wandering the fields and coastline looking for

it. Madame Proust, whose name was Madeleine, and Marcel's Aunt Léonie especially, would cook them cakes to eat during their search. Tom liked to refer to these cakes as Madeleine's cakes. The watch was never found. Many years later, Marcel wrote a book about their time together. Its title in English is "The Search for Tom's Timepiece". The French version, which was extended to cover every blade of grass in the Normandy countryside, became a best seller under the title *"À la Recherche du Temps Perdu"*.

La Santé/Health

Apparently, according to a French newspaper report, albeit some months ago, *"Emmanuel Macron prend du poids"* and *"Ça lui donne de la maturité."* Many of us could, no doubt, lose a bit of weight (*perdre du poids/maigrir*). The French, like the English, are encouraged to:

Mangez au moins cinq fruits et légumes par jour.

Évitez de manger trop gras, trop salé, trop sucré.

Évitez de grignoter entre les repas.

Pratiquez une activité physique régulière.

L'alcool, c'est maximum deux verres par jour et pas tous les jours.

There is an advert (*une pub / publicité*) on French TV promoted by Henri Le Conte (former French tennis player) and Benjamin Castaldi (French TV *animateur* and grandson of Simone Signoret) in which they encourage you to check whether you are *en surpoids* or *en obésité,* and to follow some kind of *régime* (diet) or *programme,* offered by *commejaime.fr.*

The first step is to calculate your Body Mass Index (BMI):

Comment calculer votre IMC (Indice de Masse Corporel) pour savoir si vous êtes en situation de surpoids ou en obésité?

Par exemple: Vous pesez 90 kilos; votre hauteur est 1,80 mètres.

Votre poids en kilos divisé par votre hauteur en mètres au carré: 90 / (1,80 X 1,80) = 27,80; votre IMC = 27,80.

[Your weight in kilos] divided by [(your height in metres) multiplied (by your height in metres)] = 90 / (1.80 x 1.80) = 90 / 3.24 = 27.80; your BMI is 27.80.

L'échelle IMC:

0–15 Insuffisance de poids	15–25 Normal	26–30 en surpoids	31 + en obésité

Selon l'échelle, cette personne est en surpoids. According to the scale, this person is overweight.

Que faire pour brûler des calories (to burn some calories)? *Suivre un régime* = to go on a diet; *faire du jogging* = to go jogging; *arrêter de fumer* = to stop smoking; *manger moins de pâtisseries* = to eat fewer cakes; *boire moins d'alcool etc.*

Professor David Khayat in his book *"Arrêtez de vous priver"* says *"Mieux vaut quelques kilos de trop et se sentir bien dans sa peau".*

Les Parties du Corps

	1	2	3	4	5	6	7	8	9	10	11
1	C	N	O	M	B	R	I	L	T	V	L
2	H	G	E	N	O	U	L	I	E	O	A
3	E	S	S	I	U	C	C	N	L	J	N
4	V	F	O	S	C	E	T	A	L	O	G
5	I	R	R	E	H	R	D	C	O	U	U
6	L	O	E	I	E	V	E	V	M	E	E
7	L	N	I	N	M	E	N	T	O	N	E
8	E	T	L	I	C	L	T	E	T	E	N
9	B	E	L	G	N	O	M	D	S	P	I
10	M	R	E	A	E	P	A	U	L	E	R
11	A	O	A	D	T	G	I	O	D	A	A
12	J	D	O	S	Z	E	N	C	L	U	N

In the above grid[2], there are 31 French words for human body parts. They all read in a straight line, vertically, horizontally or diagonally in all directions. The final letter of one word may also be the letter ending another. Some words will intersect others. When you have found them all and struck a line through them, you will be left with just 8 letters. Rearrange these letters to discover the name of a French *département* which is also the name of a famous alcoholic drink.

These 31 French words for human body parts, and the solution, are given in Appendix 3.

---

2 this grid has been adapted from one that appeared in Paris Match of 14th August 1981.

The English words for these body parts (in no particular order) are as follows:

mouth	lip	bone	nose	ear	breast
head	knee	nail	forehead	thigh	calf
hand	arm	back	finger	shoulder	elbow
skin	chin	tooth	neck	cheek	stomach
belly button; eyelash	nostril	leg	ankle	tongue	eye

See also Appendix 6 for some expressions with body parts.

Some 2021 topics and vocabulary

*La pandémie du coronavirus/de la Covid-19; le confinement (*lockdown*);
le déconfinement (*relaxation of lockdown measures*); les gestes barrières*
(protective measures*); la distanciation sociale d'un ou deux mètres.*
See Appendix 11 for extensive vocabulary.

*La sûreté du vaccin AstraZenica; la méfiance du vaccin AstraZenica
en Europe est-elle justifiée? Est-ce qu' il provoque des caillots* (blood
clots)?*; la pénurie des vaccins en Europe; la menace de l'UE d'arrêter
l'exportation des vaccins; la flambée du virus et du variant britannique
en Europe; une troisième vague.*

"Dedans avec les miens, dehors en citoyen", the latest French government
slogan setting out do's and don'ts for people living in the 16
départements subject to tighter Covid restrictions (23 March 2021).
See Appendix 12 for details.

Le stade de France a été transformé en <u>vaccinodrome</u> (le 6 avril 2021).

*Le premier "<u>vaccidrive</u>" de France, permettant de se faire vacciner contre
la Covid-19 sur rendez-vous, en restant dans sa voiture, a ouvert à
Montpellier (le 12 avril 2021).*

Les dîners clandestins: these are dinners arranged privately and in
secret by restaurants but in breach of Covid rules. *Les attroupements*
are unlawful gatherings of people/mobs; *des fêtes sauvages/ clandestines*
are illegal/unauthorised parties/raves.

*L'Union Européenne n'a pas renouvelé son contrat de vaccin contre la
Covid-19 avec AstraZenica pour après le mois de juin (le 9 mai 2021).
L'Inde a franchi la barre des 300.000 décès de la Covid-19 (le 24 mai
2021).*

*Vaccinations (anti-Covid-19) en France: 34.701.785 personnes ont reçu
une première injection et 24.851.829 personnes ont été vaccinées avec deux
doses. Certaines personnes ne reçoivent qu'une dose et certains vaccins
sont mono-dose (le 4 juillet 2021).*

Government-led debates/enquiries with interested parties have
been given the names of the locations of the relevant ministries

in Paris. Thus, since the *Ministère de l'Intérieur* is located *Place Beauvau*, the enquiry into *la sécurité* is called *le Beauvau de la Sécurité;* similarly, *le Grenelle de l'Environnement* and *le Ségur de la Santé*.

La sécurité is likely to be at the heart of the 2022 French Presidential Election campaign, covering a wide area of issues and concerns: *la laïcité; le port du voile / l'assimilation; le séparatisme; le communautarisme; le délitement* (division/ disintegration)*; le civisme* (good citizenship); *l'islamophobie; le terrorisme islamiste; l'islamogauchisme; les extrémistes; la délinquance; les attaques sur les forces de l'ordre / la haine anti-police; le traffic de drogues; la politique d'immigration / l'application des lois vis-à-vis des clandestins* (illegal immigrants); *le féminicide* (murder of a woman because she is a woman).

Les gilets jaunes, les black blocs, les ultras, les casseurs take part in *manifestations* (demonstrations) often descending into violence. *La canaille* scum, *la racaille* riff-raff, low-life, *les apaches / les voyous* (hooligans, gangsters).

Les rixes entre jeunes/adolescents/bandes are violent quarrels/fights between teenagers/rival gangs. *Tabasser qqn.; passer qqn. à tabac* (to beat up someone); *prendre qqn. à partie* (to attack someone); *poignarder qqn.* (to stab someone).

Les rodéos urbains are where groups of motorbikers drive around, and perform "wheelies", in town squares, endangering the public and causing a nuisance.

Une salle de shoot is a supervised drug injection centre, where drug addicts can go to inject themselves, rather than in the streets and parks.

Des tags racistes and *des tags anti-police* are, respectively, racist and anti-police graffiti.

Une marche blanche (lit. a white march) is a silent/peaceful march of sympathy or support for a victim or victims of a crime; *une arme blanche* (lit. a white weapon) is a knife or bladed weapon; *une attaque au couteau / à l'arme blanche;* [*une nuit blanche* is a sleepless night; *une paix blanche* is a peace with neither victor nor vanquished]*; un "plan blanc"* is a hospital contingency plan to deal with a significant increase in (eg. Covid) patients.

Le vapotage is *fumer une cigarette électronique; vapoter:* to vape; *un vapoteur/une vapoteuse:* a person who vapes; *une vapoteuse:* a vape pen.

Un influenceur / une influenceuse are internet influencers who promote products to their followers. See Appendix 8 for more computer / telephone related vocabulary.

Emmanuel Macron a annoncé la création d'un nouvel Institut du service public (IPS) pour remplacer l'ENA (École natonale d'administration).

Le décès du Prince Philip, duc d'Edimbourg, le 9 avril 2021, à l'âge de 99 ans (1921–2021): les drapeaux britanniques ont été mis en berne au palais de Buckingham; Elisabeth II: "Philip, c'était mon roc".

L'humour du Prince Philip: "N'oubliez pas que je suis le champion du dévoilement des plaques mémoriales".

Plusieurs centaines de milliers d'hectares de cultures (crops) *ont été impactés par le brutal épisode de gel* (frost) *qui a suivi une forte hausse des températures (début avril 2021).* See Appendix 4 for some weather vocabulary.

Le bicentenaire de la mort de Napoléon a été commémoré le 5 mai 2021.

Novak Djokovic a remporté le tournoi de Roland-Garros -son 19ème titre en Grand Chelem- en vainquant Stephanos Tsitsipas 6-7,2-6,6-3, 6-2,6-4 (le 13 juin 2021).

Les Jeux Olympiques au Japon ont eu lieu cet été sans la participation des spectateurs de l'étranger.

La prochaine élection présidentielle en France se tiendra le 10 et 24 avril 2022.

Le Tour de France 2023 partira de Bilbao au Pays basque.

Jean-Paul Belmondo, grand acteur du cinéma français et cascadeur, est mort à l'âge de 88 ans (le 6 septembre 2021).

La Britannique, Emma Raducanu, 18 ans, a remporté l'US Open, en battant en finale 6-4, 6-3, la Canadienne, Leylah Fernandez, 19 ans, à New York (le 11 septembre).

Eric Zemmour, philosophe, journaliste et écrivain, est obligé de quitter la chaîne de télévision, C News, soupconné d'être candidat, non-encore déclaré, pour l'élection présidentielle en 2022 (le 13 septembre).

Joséphine Baker (1906-1975) chanteuse, danseuse et figure de la Résistance et de la lutte antiraciste, est entrée au Panthéon le 30 novembre 2021.

PART 2

Public Signs and Notices

Tourist: Does that mean what I think
it does?
Guide: No that will be "À bas les soutiens
- gorge!"

Some Public Signs, Notices and Instructions

Being able to understand public signs and notices is a useful way of expanding your vocabulary; it is, of course, of enormous benefit in everyday life and, indeed, essential in order to comply with safety instructions and the law. Here is a selection:

Dégustation de vins

"Wine tasting". This may be preceded by *une visite aux caves* (tour of the wine cellars). There is no obligation, but you should be prepared to buy a bottle of wine or something else on offer.

Brocante

A "second-hand or antiques market" held on a public square or by the side of a road. You may also see signs for *braderie* or a *vide grenier* which are smaller sales of second-hand goods. *Les chineurs* are the people looking for bargains; *chiner* is the verb.

Métro

A *métro* station in French is *une station de métro* (you can also have *une station d'essence (petrol station), une station de ski (ski resort), une station balnéaire (seaside resort), une station spatiale (space station)).* The railway station is *la gare* as in *la Gare du Nord*, the Eurostar terminus in Paris. *La gare routière* is the bus station and the terminus for the Eurolines bus service from London Victoria is *au parc de Bercy*. Many names of Paris *métro* stations have an historical significance[3]. For example, you can access the Eiffel Tower from the *métro* stations Bir-Hakeim and Trocadéro:

---

3 For more information on the origins of names of Paris métro stations, I refer
   you to "Stations de Métro" by Gérard Roland.

| Bir-Hakeim |

This was a fortified post in Libya, about 35 miles from Tobruk, where a French brigade held out for 16 days (26th May-11th June 1942) against the German tank forces of General Rommel. This permitted the withdrawal of British troops to El Alamein and subsequent victory by General Montgomery.

| Trocadéro |

This was a fort in the Bay of Cadiz captured by the French troops of the Duke of Angoulême from Spanish insurgents on 31 August 1823. Its name was subsequently given to a building which was itself replaced by the present day *palais de Chaillot* which houses various museums including *le musée de l'Homme*.

The *métro* station closest to *les Catacombes* – an amazing underground burial ground in a disused quarry through which you can walk – not for the claustrophobic – is Denfert Rochereau:

| Denfert-Rochereau |

Pierre-Philippe Aristide Denfert-Rochereau was born at Saint-Maixent in 1823 and died in 1878. This Colonel successfully defended the town of Belfort from 1870-1871 against the Prussians; which allowed France to keep this town as part of the Peace Treaty. The defeat of France in the Franco-Prussian War led to the abdication of Napoléon III. A sculpture by Bertholdi (he who sculpted the Statue of Liberty) of the Lion of Belfort adorns the Place Denfert and recalls Denfert-Rochereau's Belfort victory.

Until 1879 this square was called *La Place d'Enfer* (Hell's Square). The entrance to the Catacombes is through an old building on the square. Above the ticket office is the following sign:

> Vous entrez ici
> dans l'Enfer
> No photo flash
> No dog

When you emerge from the Catacombes up a steep flight of stone steps – which is at the end of a 1500 metre-long route – full of neatly stacked up bones transported here from other cemeteries including from *le Cimetière des Innocents* marked today by *La Fontaine des Innocents* – the nearest *métro* station is Alésia:

> Alésia

Alésia was the name of an old gallic citadel where in 52 BC, king of the Gauls, Vercingatorix, had to surrender to Caesar after a siege of two months. This battle marked the beginning of the Gallo-Roman era. The citadel on Mount Auxois is thought to have overlooked the present day town of *Alise Sainte-Reine* in the *département de la Côte d'Or* in the *région de Bourgogne-Franche-Compté*.

Je dois rester dehors

There are signs for dogs and their owners:
A *cynophile* is a dog lover as opposed to a *cinéphile* film enthusiast.
Le cynodrome is the greyhound (*le lévrier*) racing track; similarly, *le vélodrome* (cycle-racing track) and *l'hippodrome* (horse-racing track).

This sign is in front of the Palais de Justice in Nice:

> Cette place n'est pas destinée
> à des déjections canines
> Tout abus sera passible d'une amende

Les déjections canines = les crottes de chien!

You will see lots of signs with "Défense de" and "Il est interdit de".
*Défense de fumer (*No smoking*), Défense d'entrer, Défense de cracher* (No spitting), *Défense d'afficher* (No posters).
Il est interdit de marcher sur la pelouse (Keep off the grass).

I came across the following sign in the South of France. This might have been better translated: No Parking in the Square.

> Stationnement interdit
> sur toute la place
>
> No Parking
> All over the place

Something may have broken down, not be working, or not be in service:

> En Panne

> Hors (de) service

Ma voiture est en panne; elle est chez le garagiste (une crevaison is a tyre puncture).
L'ascenseur est en panne: empruntez l'escalier.
L'électricité est en panne. Une panne d'écriture is writer's block.

Getting on a bus, you may see this sign:

> Préparer l'appoint

It means "have the right money ready" or "no change given." In *Métro* stations, you may see this sign:

> Attention aux
> vendeurs à la sauvette

Beware of ticket sellers who will offer you a *métro* ticket in the queue, thus saving you a few minutes; "*à la sauvette*" means "likely to run off" if the transport police should be around.

In main railway stations, you will see

> Consigne

This is where you can leave your luggage. *Une consigne automatique* is a left luggage locker. The word *consigne* can also mean an order/command; an instruction; and a redeemable deposit on a drinks bottle.

> Bureau des Objets Trouvés

This is the Lost Property Office.
Nearby may be the

> Syndicat d'Initiative

This is the tourist office which can also be *Le Bureau* or *L'Office de Tourisme.*

Some safety notices and road signs:

> Danger de mort

Danger of death

> Vous n'avez pas la priorité

You don't have right of way.

> Cédez le passage

Give Way

> Sens interdit

No Entry

| Sens unique |

One way

| Péage |

Motorway toll

In the back window of cars, I have seen (very occasionally) home-made signs:

| En Vadrouille |

"On Tour" or "Roaming About"

| En Villégiature |

"On holiday"

| En cas d'incendie, empruntez l'escalier |

In case of fire, take the stairs

| Zone de moustiques N'ouvrez pas la fenêtre |

Mosquitoes Don't open the window

| Pas de Sortie |

No Exit

| Remettre votre clé à la réception en sortant |

Hand in your key when leaving the hotel

| Empruntez le passage souterrain |

Take the subway/underground passageway

In shop doorways and windows – apart from *Ouvert* (open) and *Fermé* (shut):

| Entrée libre |

No obligation to buy

| Soldes |

Sales

| Liquidation |

Closing down sales – which they never are.

| Remises de 20% (discounts of 20%)
Rabais (discounts) |

| premières, secondes et dernières démarques
(1st, 2nd and final price mark downs) |

| Quincaillerie |

A hardware store

Some other signs:

| Peinture fraîche |

Wet paint

| Eau potable |

Drinking water.

| Zone fumeur |

Smoking Area

| Zone piétonne |

Pedestrian zone

| Complet |

No vacancies; full up; sold out

| S'adresser à la Direction |

Go the Admin. Office

| Vous êtes prié(e)s de vous adresser au Bureau d'Accueil |

You are requested to go to the Welcome Office/Reception

PART 3

Food, drink and hotels

Le Bouillon Chartier
7 Rue du Faubourg Montmartre 75009 Paris

On mange bien en France

Food and drink in France is generally top quality, at outdoor markets and in the supermarkets and restaurants.

Boulangerie/Pâtisserie

French bread and French pastries are second to none. Head for the nearest *boulangerie* or *pâtisserie;* or a combined *boulangerie/ pâtisserie.* The quality of freshly baked *pain, croissants and pains au chocolat* is superb. The *gâteaux* are just as good: *chaussons aux pommes, millefeuilles, flans, éclairs, tartes aux poires, tartes aux fruits, macarons...* The French for doughnuts is *les beignets.*
We are all familiar with *la baguette (de pain)* but French bread has different names (eg *ficelle, bâtard, saucisson, couronne, etc.*) depending on its thickness and shape. I was once in a Chinese restaurant when someone requested *une baguette;* which I found strange, only to find out that *une baguette* is also a pair of chopsticks. Harry Potter's magic wand is *une baguette magique.*
Baguette *sandwich(e)s (*pronounced *sond weesh) au fromage, au jambon beurre, au poulet, campagnard* are top quality too. In Nice, try *les pans bagnats* and *socca.*

Cafés, bars, restaurants, bistrots, brasseries, estaminets, crêperies

If you order a coffee (*un café*) you will get a black coffee, and probably a one shot expresso (*un expresso*). For a coffee with milk, you must request *un café crème.* If you want a large one, then *un grand crème.* You can also request *un cappuccino.* In the south of France, *un café noisette* is a small coffee with a dash of cream. A *café au lait* is usually a bowl of milky coffee served at breakfast time. If you stand at the bar (*le zinc or le comptoir*) and drink your coffee, it will be cheaper than if you sit down at a table and order. You can request *la note* (the bill for drinks) as opposed to *l'addition* (the bill for a full-blown restaurant meal).

To attract the attention of the waiter (*serveur/garçon*) or waitress (*serveuse*), it is best to gently say: "*S'il vous plaît Madame*" or "*Mademoiselle*" or "*Monsieur*". I would hesitate to shout out: "*Garçon!*", as if you were calling your pet labrador to heel. French waiters can be a bit tetchy, especially in Paris.

If you do not want to pay for bottled water in a restaurant, and you are having a meal, you can request *une carafe d'eau* or *une carafe d'eau du robinet* / a jug of tap water. If you do want bottled water, you may want *une bouteille d'eau minérale gazeuse ou naturelle* (a bottle of sparkling or non-sparkling mineral water). *De l'eau pétillante* or *de l'eau plate* also mean sparkling or non-sparkling water.

Est-ce que le service est compris?
Do I need to leave a tip (un pourboire)?

When it comes to paying the bill for a restaurant meal, the price is *le prix net* which means service, usually of around 15% maximum, is included. The amount of the service charge is clearly indicated on the bill and should also have been clearly stated on the menu (*la carte*).

So, there should be no surprise. You pay the *prix net* as indicated. You are under no obligation to leave an additional tip. Some waiters will try to convince you that the service charge (*le service*) is not the tip (*le pourboire*). Only if you have received exceptional service or had an exceptional meal, should you consider leaving an additional *pourboire* for the waiter or waitress.

Of course, if you are unhappy with your meal and the service provided, you will have a job to get the service charge removed.

But, at the very least, check the bill with a fine tooth-comb to make sure you are only being charged for the items you ordered. Make sure you communicate politely your dissatisfaction: *"C'est pas possible! Nous ne payons pas le service"*. But don't say: *"Ma soupe vichyssoise était froide"*, even if it was cold, because it is supposed to be served chilled!

If you are really unhappy, you can make your feelings clear by saying: *"Nous ne reviendrons jamais ici!"* (We are never coming back here!); *"Voleurs!"* (Thieves!) may be one step too far. I did once suggest to a restaurant owner in Paris, and to all his other customers present, that he should put a notice in his window *"Ici on roule les touristes étrangers"* ("In here we rip off foreign tourists!"). I was part of a group of friends and colleagues. The waiter did not know we could all speak French reasonably well. The food was not good, the service was extremely slow, and the bill was inflated with items we had not even ordered. So much for *le sang-froid anglais*; we were fuming!

For Whom the Bill Tolls?

I was in Normandy with a friend of mine. We were on a trip to visit some of the major sites of the D-Day landing beaches (*les plages du débarquement*). See Appendix 1 for our itinerary. We took the opportunity to visit my friend's French cousin and wife who live in Ouistreham, the port of arrival of the Portsmouth–Caen ferry. Whilst with his cousin, we visited the site of the German gun battery at Merville which was put out of action by British troops of the 9th Parachute Battalion led by Lt. Col. Terence Otway, prior to the beach landings on 6th June 1944; and then we all went for lunch at a restaurant by the sea at Cabourg. We sat at an outside table; *en terrasse* would be too good a description. My friend had told me that he did not want his cousin to pay for the meal; he himself would pay for all of us. The cousin took control at the restaurant; he and his wife being native French speakers. We had a very nice meal. We ordered dessert and coffee at the same time to speed up the service. After dessert, and waiting for the coffees, my friend got up and said he was going to *les WC*. He went inside. I knew he was going to pay the bill. He came back about five minutes later, sat down, and said nothing. The coffee finally arrived. The cousin downed his *expresso* in one, got up and said he was going to *les toilettes*. Five minutes later, the cousin came back, smiling, and declared that he had just paid the bill: *"Vous êtes tous invités; l'addition est réglée!"* I looked at my friend. There was a look of terror on his face. He babbled: *"Mais, ce n'est pas possible! I paid the bill over fifteen minutes ago!"*. Cousin and friend went back inside the restaurant. The "mistake" was recognised. One big problem remained: how to reimburse one of the credit cards and to whom. I am sure the delay in resolving the matter was owing more to a discussion between my friend and his cousin, than the "technical problem" which was the explanation given to me and the cousin's wife.

I said, "I don't know who has finally paid the bill, but thank you for the meal."

Food, Glorious Food!
La Grande Bouffe

For fish, it is *du poisson* and not *du poison*. I once saw on a menu -*la roussette*- with the English translation of dog-fish; had they called it huss or rock salmon I might have been ever so slightly more tempted; we dissected dogfish in our biology class at school. If you are by a fishing port in France, then do try *une assiette de fruits de mer* (all sorts of different shellfish: *homard, langoustines, crabe, crevettes, moules, huîtres, coquilles Saint- Jacques*); and the fish, particularly *le bar* (sea bass) *la daurade* (sea bream) and *le turbot*. Nîmes is noted for its *brandade de morue* (a salted cod speciality); and in Sète you should sample the take-away (*à emporter*) *tielle de pieuvre/poulpe* (octopus pie) from an establishment called Sophie Cianni & Co.

Fresh fruit in France is so good:
*Les melons, les pastèques (*water melons*), les fraises* (strawberries), *les framboises* (raspberries), *les raisins* (grapes), *les pêches, les pommes* (apples)…
Une fraise is a strawberry; it's also the word for a *dentist's drill* and *fraiser une dent is* to drill a tooth.
France has so many good cheeses *(fromages)*; my favourites are some of the Normandy cheeses: *camembert, brie* and *pont l'évêque*. I don't like the blue cheeses or indeed any of the goat cheeses (*fromages de chèvre*). *Général de Gaulle* once posed the rhetorical question: "How can you govern a country which produces so many cheeses? A *croque-monsieur* or a *croque-madame* (toasted ham and cheese sandwich with an egg on top) can be quite filling.
As an *hors-d'oeuvre*, I recommend *une assiette de crudités*, a plate of raw chopped salad vegetables *(carottes rapées, betteraves, salade de chou cru (coleslaw etc.)*. Of course, as an alternative, you might like to try some *fromage de chèvre* or *6 escargots*. Snails can be a bit chewy for my liking and they are cooked in garlic butter and parsley. Check out *le potage du jour (soupe à l'oignon, soupe au pistou, soupe*

vichyssoise (<u>chilled</u> creamy vegetable soup); *bisque* is a shellfish soup and *la bouillabaisse* a very filling *provençal* fish soup. There is always *cocktail de crevettes* (prawn cocktail) and *pâté de foie gras*; *terrine* and *rillettes* are other types of *pâtés* or potted meat.

The French know how to make *omelettes*. If you are tired of *steak frites*, you can always ask for *une omelette* (*au jambon, au fromage, mixte fromage et jambon, mixte fromage – jambon – champignons), garnie de salade* (with lettuce) or *avec frites*. The fluffy omelette which is *l'omelette de la mère Poulard* served in restaurants on *Mont St Michel* is, however, an acquired taste. *Poulet et frites (chicken and chips)* is another good alternative. Noodles are *les nouilles* (rhymes with *la grenouille* (frog)); and *les cuisses de grenouille* are frogs legs not seen on many menus nowadays; and *les pâtes* are pasta -*les spaghetti, nouilles, macaronis,* etc.

Les (pommes de terre) frites are chips/French fries; *les chips* (pronounced *sheeps*) are crisps. *Les champignons comestibles* are mushrooms like *chanterelles* and *cèpes*; *les champignons mortels et non-comestibles* are poisonous funghi or toadstools.

Attention – unless you like tripe, and quite frankly who does, <u>stay well clear of</u> *andouillettes* (pigs intestines); *boudin noir* (blood sausage), *boudin blanc (*may contain chicken amongst other things*);* and *cervelle de mouton* and *cervelle de veau* (sheep's and calf's brain). I would also add *langue de boeuf* (tongue) to this list of *comestibles à éviter*.

Crêperies

If you can find a *crêperie*, you can have savoury-filled *galettes/ crêpes au sarasin* (buckwheat pancakes) washed down with *un verre de cidre* (a glass of cider) or *un pichet de cidre* (a small jug of cider); and for dessert, *crêpes au froment* (flour-based pancakes) just *sucrées*, or filled with *banane* (banana), *glaces* (ice-cream), *crème chantilly*, *confiture* (jam) or *Nutella* (chocolate spread).

Les desserts

On *desserts*, more generally, the fairly typical ones are *mousse au chocolat, crème caramel, tarte tatin*[4], *tarte du jour* or *tarte du moment* (usually *tarte aux pommes* or *tarte aux poires*), *deux boules de glace vanille (other parfums* (flavours) include *fraise, framboise* (raspberry), *citron, pistache...).*

Mousse au chocolat à volonté

If you should see on a menu that something is *à volonté*, it generally means *as much as you can eat*.

I was having a meal once in a Belgian restaurant with two colleagues. They ordered something like *tarte aux pommes* and *crème caramel*. I decided to order the *mousse au chocolat à volonté*. Their desserts arrived almost immediately, mine took a little longer. I had my back to the waitress. Finally, it was on its way. My two colleagues had a broad smile on their faces. Instead of serving me a normal portion of *mousse* in a small glass and then subsequently bringing me additional amounts as I required, a dinner-plateful of what looked like a cow pat (*bouse de vache*) was put down in front of me. I stared at it in disbelief. My two colleagues, by this time, were in fits of laughter. One said it looked like *merde* (shit). All three of us were *pris d'un fou rire*, that mad hysterical laughter which, however hard you try, you can only suppress for a few seconds before you are set off again. I tried one mouthful of that *mousse*; I could not eat it. I told the waitress I had lost my appetite. We laughed all the way back to our hotel.

---

4 In Appendix 2 you will find a recipe for tarte tatin.

Quelques boissons / Some drinks

Un diabolo has fizzy lemonade in it: un *diabolo menthe (a green drink); un diabolo fraise (a red drink); un diabolo grenadine. Une grenade* means both a (hand-) grenade and a pomegranate. *Un citron pressé* is a bitter lemon drink. *Une limonade* will not necessarily get you a fizzy lemonade. It is best to ask for *un Fanta limonade* or *un Sprite.* *Un Orangina* is a well-known fizzy orange drink.

Une bière (à la) pression is a draught beer: un demi is a pint; *un galopin* is a small beer (in the Hôtel Ibis Centre Toulouse at least). You can simply ask *for une grande or petite bière (pression or en bouteille).* *Une bière en bouteille: une bouteille de 1664, de Heineken, de Pils, de Peroni.*

Un demi panaché is a pint of shandy.

Les eaux de vie are spirits: *un whisky (un scotch), un cognac, un armagnac, un calvados (*apple brandy*); la fée verte* is *l'absinthe* legally sold in France.

Les liqueurs: une Chartreuse, une Bénédictine.

Un pastis, un Ricard, or *un Pernod* is an aniseed-based *apéritif* drink.

Un kir is a blackcurrent juice (*cassis*) and white wine (*vin blanc);* and *un kir royal* is *cassis* and champagne (*du champagne*); *un mimosa* is a cocktail (*un cocktail*) which is a mixture of orange juice (*jus d'orange*) and *champagne* rather like a Buck's fizz.

Un café irlandais is an Irish coffee in principle; *c'est-à-dire que* some places know how to make a good one and others do not.

Un pousse-café is a drop of *cognac* or *calvados* to go with your coffee = *le trou normand; une bistouille* is a coffee fortified with a drop of brandy and usually drunk as a *digestif.*

Un ballon de rouge is a (quickly taken) glass of cheap red wine to help a workman on his way in the morning. That's <u>not</u> to say that *les éboueurs français sont des alcooliques* (French refuse collectors are not alcoholics)!

Every French wine connoisseur *(connaisseur/ bluffeur)* believes that the English know that there are really only three French wines: *rouge, blanc* and *rosé;* including a fizzy white one called *champagne.* If you cannot decide on which *appellation contrôlée/*

grand cru wine to select from the expensive *carte des vins,* you can opt for *un verre de vin* or *un pichet de vin de (la) maison (25cl, 50cl, 75cl)- (rouge, blanc or rosé)* which is usually a reasonably priced and drinkable *vin de table.*

If you order a bottle of wine in a restaurant, the waiter will pour out a little drop for one of you to try. This can lead to fun and games as to who is going to sample the wine, and what sort of performance they are going to put on. The French can always put on a first-class performance and love to undertake this little pre-food ceremony. They will fight to take the lead role as if they are Gérard Depardieu himself. The proud chosen one picks up the glass, sniffs it, waits at least twenty seconds, swirling the wine in the glass, and then takes a taste that lingers on the tongue for another twenty seconds. Everyone is gripped in suspense, anxiously waiting for the verdict. A French declaration is made: *"Le bouquet… est comme la fragrance du Chanel n°5; et, sincèrement, le goût… Le goût me rappelle les meilleurs fruits français de l'été que ma chère pauvre mère cueillait tous les ans dans les champs de Provence ensoleillés".* And everyone is filled with emotion and applauds as the waiter fills every glass. The waiter too is overcome. *"We, French people, we are so knowledgeable and refined,"* he thinks to himself in perfect English.

An English group faced with the same task is put on the spot. Usually, the head of the family or the person paying for the wine will have to be the chosen one.

There's a discussion: *"You try it".*

"No, you try it".

"You ordered it; you taste it."

"No, you do it."

"I don't want to."

"I'm your dad, not flipping Gérard Depardieu".

The reluctant chosen one, perhaps the second or third choice, picks up the glass containing the sample, looks at it, downs it in one and turns to the waiter and says, *"Yes, that's ok"* (or even *"Oui, c'est bon").* The waiter fills up all the glasses and departs in silence.

Another member of the group picks up his full glass, takes a sip and declares: *"It tastes like ditch- water."* And everyone falls about laughing.

Le sommelier is a wine waiter. *Les caves* or *les chais* are cellars. *L'oenologie* is the science of wine and *un oenophile* is a wine lover. *"J'ai trop bu. Où sont les toilettes?"* is *"I've drunk too much. Where are the toilets?"; "Je suis soûl(e)"* or *"Je suis paf"* (I am drunk); *"Il boit comme un trou"* (he drinks too much) and *"Je vais me soûler"* (I'm going to get drunk). *"Elle est alcoolique"* (she's an alcoholic). And as JR Ewing from Dallas famously said: *"Ne me mens pas, Sue Ellen, je sais que tu t'es remise à boire"* (Don't lie to me, Sue Ellen, I know you've started to drink again). And, as Sue Ellen was learning French, she said to Cliff Barnes: *"Si nous allions prendre un pot quelque part?"* (Suppose we go and have a drink somewhere?). And Cliff didn't know what she was on about. So, he took her out to his favourite *troquet* for a drink. Next morning around midday, Sue Ellen finally surfaces: *"J'ai mal aux cheveux"* (I've got a hang-over). JR replies, "Your hair is a mess too".

Les Hôtels

I have often wondered whether anyone has tried to book a room (*une chambre*) in *l'Hôtel de Ville* (the town or city hall) or *l'Hôtel des Monnaies* (the Royal Mint). A *hôtel particulier* is a town house or mansion, rather than a hotel. Such buildings are privately owned or occupied by public services such as libraries and museums. In Paris, *l'hôtel Biron* is the *Musée Rodin* and *l'hôtel Salé* is the *Musée Picasso*. *L'Hôtel des Impôts* is the tax office (*le Bureau de Perception* sounds just as nice) and *l'Hôtel de Police* can be a police station (though a police station is more usually *le commissariat de police* or *la gendarmerie*). The oldest hospital (*l'hôpital*) in Paris is *L'Hôtel-Dieu* situated near the cathedral of *Notre-Dame*. *L'hôtel de Matignon* is the official residence of the French prime minister.

L'Hôtel des Invalides in Paris is a hospital which was set up, under the reign of Louis XIV, to house and care for injured war veterans; and this building complex and the Palais de Versailles are his outstanding monuments in Paris. *L'Église du Dôme de l'Hôtel des Invalides* houses *le tombeau de l'Empereur Napoléon I* (Napoleon's tomb).

Napoleon apparently said, "You are only as great as the buildings you leave behind." (Or was it George Pompidou or François Mitterrand?).

Napoleon commissioned the *Arc de Triomphe* to commemorate his great victories. The first he saw of it was, posthumously, when his body was brought back from St Helena in 1840, in a ship called *La Belle Poule* on his way eventually to his final resting place. Though designed in 1806, the Arc de Triomphe was not completed until 1836. Napoleon died in exile in 1821 and to this day some French people believe he was poisoned by the British. The bicentenary of Napoleon's death was on 5 May 2021.

Close to the Emperor's tomb, beneath a stone slab, rests the body of *Napoléon II*, the Duke of Reichstadt, son of Napoleon from his second marriage to Marie Louise of Austria. When Napoleon was exiled to St Helena she took her son back to Vienna. He was a sickly child and died aged 21 in 1832. When Germany occupied France (1940-1944) in the Second World War, as a magnanimous gesture of camaraderie, or so he thought, Adolf Hitler had the body of *Napoléon II* repatriated to France.

In 1870 France was defeated in the Franco-Prussian War. The *Empereur Napoléon III*, nephew of *Napoléon I*, abdicated and came to live in England. He and his wife, the Empress Eugénie, and their son the Prince Imperial (also known as *Napoléon IV*) rest in the Imperial Crypt in a mausoleum at St Michael's Abbey in Farnborough, Hampshire. The granite sarcophagi were provided by Queen Victoria. *Napoléon III's* most famous building legacy is the magnificent *Opéra Garnier* in Paris. The architect, Charles Garnier, was not officially invited to the opening ceremony. The building was completed only after the abdication of Napoleon III. It was officially opened in 1875 and the then President, *Maréchal Mac-Mahon*, of the new Third Republic did not want to associate himself with the previous regime. Garnier apparently bought his own entry ticket to the ceremony.

L'Hôtel du Nord

The Hôtel du Nord was a family-run hotel on the edge of the Canal St Martin in Paris. It is immortalised in Marcel Carné's film of the same name, shot in black and white in 1938. The film stars Louis Jouvet and features Arletty. Both were to star in Carné's film "Les Enfants du Paradis" in 1945. Hôtel du Nord was not, however, filmed on location; though you would not believe so, even today, if you visit the actual Hôtel site and Canal. An expensive set was made at the Billancourt, Paris Studios, reproducing a 70 metre stretch of the Canal St Martin, a footbridge and the Hôtel du Nord. Arletty's minor role as Raymonde in this film gained attention for the now famous line:

"Atmosphère! Atmosphère! Est-ce que j'ai une gueule d'atmosphère?"
(Do I look like the kind of girl that wants atmosphere?).
Arletty was imprisoned for 18 months in 1945 for her wartime *liaison* with a German Luftwaffe officer. Most of her sentence was spent in a private *château*. She later is supposed to have said in her defence: *"Mon coeur est français, mais mon cul est international."* Arletty, whose real name was Léonie Marie Julie Bathiat, died in 1992 at the age of 94. One of her last screen appearances was in a small role as an elderly French woman in The Longest Day (1962).

Le petit déjeuner en chambre

I had just arrived early evening in Brussels and went to register for one night at a medium-sized three-star hotel. There was a notice in reception giving you the option of having *petit déjeuner en chambre ou en salle entre 6h00 et 10h00*. Since I wanted to get away early the next morning, I asked the receptionist if I could order breakfast in my room.

She said, to do so, I would have to go to my room and ring reception. I replied: "But, you are in reception?"

"Yes", she said.

I went to my room and rang reception. I said: "It's me".

"Yes it's you," she replied.

I said, "I would like to order breakfast in my room".

"Ha ha ha", she laughed. "But Monsieur, you cannot have breakfast tonight."

"Ha ha ha," I laughed back. "But Mademoiselle, I do not want breakfast tonight. I want to order breakfast in my room for tomorrow morning. I am going out shortly for dinner."

"Monsieur," she replied, "you must ring this number tomorrow morning and ask the receptionist to bring breakfast to your room." I did not persist. More mutual ha ha ha's as I left the hotel to go out for dinner. Next morning, my alarm went off at 6 a.m. I rang reception. After a few minutes, a man replied. I posed the question.

He said, "Monsieur, I am very busy. I have to manage reception and look after the breakfast room. I am very sorry. Can you *descend* for breakfast as you are awake?"

I could not argue. I was indeed awake. He was obviously feeling the pressure. I had a shower, got dressed and *descended* at about 6.50 a.m. There was no-one in reception. The breakfast room was deserted. I helped myself to as many *croissants* as I could eat, cut a portion of baguette, took some butter and jam, a banana, an orange juice and a cup of coffee from a machine. I ate my breakfast alone in the *salle du petit déjeuner*. Not a soul appeared. *Pas un chat.* I *ascended* back to my room. About 8.15 a.m. I got my suitcase and went down to check out. Nobody in reception; one or two people in the breakfast room. I rang the bell. A man arrived. "Good morning, sir. Did you enjoy your breakfast?" "Yes, thank you," I said. I paid the bill and left, with a reciprocal: "*Bonne journée!*"

PART 4

Schoolboy Linguistics

ENGLISH SCHOOLBOY; "Le ciel est bleu. Les oiseaux chantent. La plume de ma tante est sur la table"

FRENCH SCHOOLBOY: "My tailor is rich. My flowers are beautiful"

Schoolboy Linguistics

Why did we have to try to learn French? Learning to read and write in English was hard enough. None of us in my class, on starting secondary school, had been to France. There was an English boy in another class whose surname was Beauchamp which he, himself, pronounced Beecham. But the French teacher always addressed him as *beau champ* (beautiful field). There was also a boy at the school whose mother was French, and he could speak French better than he could write it.

My first experience of meeting a real French person, outside of school, was when a French boy came to stay with the family of an older boy with whom we were friends. Amongst other things, we would play cricket with this older boy, usually after school in a farmer's field close to where we lived. He always batted first. It was his bat. If we got him out quickly, he would threaten to go home immediately and take his bat, unless we gave him at least three chances. Also, since we had no cricket pads, and we were playing with a hard cricket ball, we had to bowl slowly to him. When he bowled at us, he bowled as fast as he could. And when we did get him out for the third time, and it was my turn to bat, he would, often as not, say he had to go home for his tea; and he took his bat with him. It was this boy's family who were getting paid to accommodate a French boy. Our friend with the bat told the French boy, an older teenager like himself and just as rough at the edges but French- speaking, that it was okay to pee in the street provided he did so against a lamp-post. The French boy duly obliged by peeing against the lamp-post outside our house. Also, during his stay, he had been taken to the local park by his host and encouraged to shout English obscenities as loud as he could. Those two got on like a house on fire; *ils étaient amis comme cochons*. On another occasion, an older teenage French girl came to stay with a different family in our road. She was quite attractive and wore nice perfume and clothes. But she had the hint of a moustache

and an abundance of hair under her armpits. She was not a patch on that goddess Brigitte Bardot, clad in a bikini and sunbathing on a beach on the French Riviera (*la Côte d'Azur*), whose pictures we had seen, and subsequently looked for at every opportunity, in the pages of back numbers of Paris Match strewn about the classroom. As part of our French lesson, while the teacher marked some homework, we were allowed ten minutes to peruse those Paris Match magazines "to see how much we could understand". Well, of course, we could really only understand the pictures of gorgeous bikini-clad women and the pictures of French *pop stars, acteurs* and *actrices*. This is how I first came to know of Johnny Hallyday and Sylvie Vartan, Jane Birkin, Françoise Hardy, Sacha Distel, Charles Aznavour, Yves Montand, Simone Signoret, Fernandel; and Louis de Funès who was a sort of French Sid James. In the late 1960s, Sacha Distel compèred a Saturday night entertainment programme on the BBC. At school we used to mimic him singing:
"Rrain dwops keep fallin on my ead. Ah yes, zose rrain dwops keep fallin, yes zey keep fallin…"
He was very popular at the time. My mum loved him. My dad thought he was a smarmy Frenchman.
I think both Charles Aznavour and Françoise Hardy appeared as guests on the show. An Australian folk group called The Seekers would certainly have appeared. They had four or five hit songs (*des tubes*) in quick succession. My dad loved the lead singer, Judith Durham; her voice was as pure and distinctive as that of Karen Carpenter's. Our family was a little sad when they sang "The Carnival is over" for the last time and went back to Australia. A couple of years ago, at a garage sale in Hayling Island, I purchased some old vinyl LPs; one was Sacha Distel's greatest hits and another one was hit songs of The Seekers.
In the early 1960s, we used to look forward to going to "Saturday morning pictures" at the local ABC cinema. We roared with laughter at Laurel and Hardy (who we called Fatty and Skinny). A main feature film was shown each week and the stars were all American: notably Clint Eastward, John Wayne, Charlton Heston, Yul Brynner and Elvis Presley. The cinema was jammed packed just with kids,

at least two to three hundred of us. One Saturday, the manager threatened to throw us all out if we didn't stop stamping our feet to the Dave Clark Five hit song "Glad All Over", Boomp Boomp (Stamp your feet), "Yes I'm", Boomp Boomp (Stamp your feet), "Glad all Over, Baby I'm", Boomp Boomp (Stamp your feet), "Glad all over", Boomp Boomp (Stamp your feet), "Glad your mine!" Among the very first films I saw at the rival Odeon cinema were: Cliff Richard in "Summer Holiday", Elvis Presley in "Kid Gloves", the Beatles in "Hard Day's Night"; "Carry on Taxi" and "Carry on Camping" with Sid James and co., including, in the latter film, Barbara Windsor breathing out energetically and catapulting her *soutien-gorge* across *le camping*; you could say of her that *il y avait du monde au balcon*.

In the news, I was aware that President Kennedy had been shot and then later in 1968 his brother, Robert; and also, a black man called Martin Luther King. We wanted Sonny Liston to knock out that "loud-mouth" Cassius Clay. He didn't. Henry Cooper nearly knocked him out in a fight in London. Henry got a bad eye-cut, and the fight was stopped. The next morning, on the front of our national tabloid, I remember being shocked by a full-page picture of a blood-splattered Henry. Henry became a hero. Clay became Mohammed Ali, and we grew to like him. He really could "float like a butterfly and sting like a bee". He probably was "The Greatest". His fights with Smokin' Joe Frazier were brutal. Jimmy Greaves, Bobby Charlton, George Best and Denis Law, and Pele from Brazil, were the best footballers. We listened to the 1964 Tokyo Olympics on the wireless (= the radio). Mary Rand won the gold medal in the long jump; and when Anne Packer won the gold medal in the 800 metres, the commentator, David Coleman, nearly lost his voice with emotion and excitement. In 1969, Neil Armstrong was the first man to set foot on the surface of the moon: "One small step for a man; one giant leap for mankind". Mary Hopkin sang: "Those were the days my friend…" Looking back it was, as the French might say, *le temps des cerises*.

School Trip to Paris

My mum and dad scraped together enough money to send me on a school trip to Paris. I was 12 years old. It was April 1966. Until then, my only overseas trip had been to the Isle of Wight. There were no mobile phones, no computers and no internet. The Channel Tunnel did not exist. At home, we listened to the wireless. It wasn't until two months later that we rented our first television; so, we were able to watch the Football World Cup tournament, albeit in black and white. England won. Geoff Hurst scored a hat trick *(il a marqué un triplé)* in the final at Wembley Stadium. There was of course no VAR so that dodgy goal stood. A few months later, my home town team Horsham reached the first round proper of the FA Cup. They were drawn at home (Queen Street) against Swindon Town. The Health and Safety rules were not so strict in those days; additional temporary stands were erected and over 7,000 spectators, including my brother and me, watched the match which Horsham lost 3-0.

The trip to Paris was a maiden voyage for the school at the initiative of our French teacher. We took a coach from the school to Newhaven. We transferred to the Newhaven-Dieppe Ferry and the crossing took over four hours. We then transferred to a train to Paris. A coach was waiting for us at *Gare St. Lazare* to take us to the *Lycée St. Louis, Boulevard St. Michel*. We were a group of 20 boys accompanied by the French teacher, her husband who was one of the maths' teachers; and the Deputy Head Master of our Secondary Modern School who was a lot like the Windsor Davies sergeant-major character in "It Ain't Half Hot Mum". He even had a handle-bar moustache. His bark was worse than his bite (and I do mean bite, not the French *bite* pronounced *beet* which means *pénis*. See list of *Gros Mots*/swear words in Appendix 13). There must have been at least five other English school groups in the same *lycée*. We came into contact with them when we went to the communal toilets, shower rooms and dining room. The groups of girls and women teachers were all accommodated on a different floor. Our group of 20 slept in one big dormitory along with Windsor Davies. The French teacher and her husband, so we believed, were staying in a hotel across the road but they may just have been on a different floor.

The communal toilets were disgusting, just holes in the ground and a place to put your feet. There was human excrement everywhere. The stench was awful. I don't think the toilets were cleaned once while we were there. We had not been trained to use such primitive facilities. You needed to squat over the hole for several minutes, your feet correctly in position, with trousers around your ankles and toilet paper just out of reach. In any case, to be successful in your posterior trajectory, you would have needed the leg muscles of a weight lifter, a permanently bunged up nose to avoid asphyxiation, and exceptionally long arms to reach *le papier hygiénique*. The day we went to Versailles, we had lunch in another *lycée* and, rather than eat, everyone queued for the toilets which were more modern with toilet seats. Outside our *lycée*, about 100 yards down Boulevard St. Michel, there was a public urinal. It was a circular metal affair, at the bottom of which you could see the trouser legs of the men inside. I learned that such *urinoirs* were also called *pissoirs,* and also a more distinguished name *vespasiennes* after a Roman emperor. This particular urinal exuded a pungent smell of urine. But it was like a beacon. Coming back from sightseeing, you knew you were nearly home when you could either smell or see this work of public art. It has long since been removed. Imagine putting one of those in the middle of Oxford Street!

During the day, we were taken out sightseeing; but late afternoon, an hour or so before it got dark, and before dinner, we were given free time to explore the area near the *lycée*. We went to three main places: a *boulangerie* in a backstreet on the same side of the road, which was visible from our dormitory window, where we could buy coca cola, *baguettes de pain* and *tablettes de chocolat* to share in the dormitory; across the road in the Place de la Sorbonne was a *tabac* that we called Jim Waterman's where we could purchase postcards and stamps; and further up the road was the *Jardin du Luxembourg*. There is a *bassin* in the *Jardin* just behind *le Palais du Luxembourg* (seat of the French *sénat* – their House of Lords) where you could hire small yachts and push them about with sticks. After a few evenings, we had *gendarmes*- twirling white truncheons and blowing whistles- stopping us from crossing the road until they said so; and once the yachts had drifted into the centre of the *bassin* and were irretrievable, some boys used their boat sticks to try to spear the huge carp floating near the sides and surface. *Les Anglais* were summarily banned from hiring boats from then on, but we still went to the gardens. Some boys were buying flick knives, freely on sale, and others bought cigarettes to smoke in *le Jardin*. One boy brought back to the dormitory a live lizard purchased from a pet shop. Windsor Davies twisted his ear and made him go straight back to the pet shop. That lizard was, however, let loose in the *Jardin du Luxembourg*.

One evening at communal dinner with all the other groups, the noise was, as it usually was, absolutely deafening. You had to shout to the person sitting next to you if you wanted to have a conversation. Windsor Davies had had enough. He had a short fuse anyway. He did not suffer fools gladly. He got up, stood on his chair and bellowed for everybody to shut up; because he, Windsor Davies, could not hear himself speak. By complexion he was red-faced anyway, now he was firing on all cylinders like a provoked dragon. The room went quiet. He appealed for silence in his usual, aggressive, non-diplomatic manner. A teacher from another school got up and told him to shut up himself; "it was dinner time, and everyone needed to let off steam before lights out." There was huge applause and laughter. Not from our school. Windsor was in our dormitory. If we had laughed or made any wise-cracks, he would have beaten the shit out of us, not physically but certainly verbally. The noise recommenced. He sat down deflated. His armour had been pierced that day.

Before lights out, we would play cards until the cheating got to the point where recriminations were made, and pillow fights permitted. We were encouraged to write postcards. I think Windsor thought we were a platoon of soldiers in the making and he was in charge of training us. Windsor's bed was on a slightly raised platform and he had his own light. So, after he had declared lights out, he continued to read in bed with the aid of his personal electricity supply. It also permitted him just enough light to see that there was nothing amiss in the barracks. One evening, I noticed the book he was reading: "Funny ha ha and Funny Peculiar". Even at my age I thought it might be dodgy, but I was wrong. I have to say we were a happy group, if a little unruly at times.

I think I was probably one of the very few who was interested in learning some French. Windsor certainly showed no interest.

Discipline

During the day, Windsor relied on the French teacher as much as did all the rest of us. At school he doubled as a maths teacher but his forte, as Deputy Head, was discipline. He patrolled the corridors like a prison warder; and he controlled his maths classes with a metaphorical iron rod "because you are damn well going to stay awake, pay attention and learn something." He could dish out lines and use a cane, like he was a swashbuckling *d'Artagnan*, whenever he thought the situation required it. For all that, you couldn't dislike him. He had a certain charm, and he was generally respected. He demanded to be respected. You would describe him "as old school", like much of our school building.

Paris in April 1966 had an edge to it. Probably because I was only 12 and it was a foreign country. I was at an impressionable age. *Le Général de Gaulle* was *le Président,* and *Georges Pompidou* was *le Premier ministre.* We never saw either of them. [I wanted *Georges Pompidou* to be married to a *Madame de Pompadour*, but I found out later that they were centuries apart, even though they did both once occupy the presidential Elysée palace. The latter was mistress and then confidante of King Louis XV. In 1753 the King purchased the Hôtel d'Evreux -now known as the Elysée Palace- for her to use as a place to stay while visiting Paris]. The public phone system was not good. One evening, when we were in a café, our French teacher organised for us to buy *jetons* from the barman so we could make a telephone call home from the phone in the corner of the café. I managed to speak to my dad for about half a minute.

French money *(la monnaie française)* was confusing. There were old franc coins (*pièces d'anciens francs*) and new franc coins (*pièces de nouveaux francs*) in circulation. The old franc coins were much lighter than the new ones and apparently nearly worthless. I had a few new notes (*billets*) and a pocketful of mainly those lightweight old coins which were still being given as change (*de la monnaie*). Sometimes we had a coach to take us sightseeing. We had a trip round Paris at night to see the city lit up; and a trip on a *bateau-mouche* on the river Seine. I remember us all getting out of the coach in front of *Les Invalides*. Led by the French teacher we walked, two by two, straight in to see Napoleon's tomb. I think we stayed less than 20 minutes and then we went off to *le Palais de Versailles*, stopping at that more modern *lycée* for lunch and toilets. I cannot remember much about Versailles, except inside it was so crowded, and we were wedged in like sardines, going from room to room. Bearing in mind, I was only about three feet tall at that age, I couldn't see much except the ceilings. It was stifling and claustrophobic. I am sure we would have been told that Louis XIV used to live there but I honestly cannot remember. We must have gone in the magnificent Hall of Mirrors (*la Galérie des Glaces* which could also be translated as the "ice cream parlour") but it left no impression on me.

We went to the Louvre and saw the Mona Lisa. She smiled. We went up to *Montmartre* to visit *Sacré Coeur* and the artists' quarter around *Place du Tertre*. Some boys, those with a lot more money, had their portraits sketched. We were walked down to *Notre-Dame* and the Latin Quarter where we could do serious souvenir shopping. We walked up part of the *Champs Elysées* to the *Arc de Triomphe* and we crossed the roundabout known as *L'Étoile* to the centre to see the tomb of the unknown soldier.

We took the *Métro* on several days. That was exciting; and a challenge to quickly open the carriage doors when getting in and out. There was a distinctive *odeur* on the platforms. It wasn't unpleasant but I was informed it was probably a mixture of perfume, urine and smoke from *Gaulloises* cigarettes. Smoking was allowed everywhere. I didn't smoke.

And then the *pièce de la résistance*. We got let out of the coach near the *Trocadéro métro* station. We walked past what was then *le Musée national des Monuments Français and le Musée du Cinéma* in the west wing of the *Palais de Challiot*, and took a left turn, and Wow! Wow! Wow! *La Tour Eiffel*. Magnificent. It was rusty brown! We stayed there on the viewing platform for about half an hour. I did not own a camera. We walked down the steps and down to the river. As we crossed the *Pont d'Iéna*, there was a man with a monkey on his shoulder. For a few francs you could have your picture taken with the monkey. I didn't; some did. Of course, we went up the Eiffel Tower.

As for learning French, my teacher made me go up to a complete stranger in the *Boulevard St. Michel* and ask him the time. I did so reluctantly. *"Excusez-moi. Quelle heure est-il?,"* I said. He replied; and I said, *"Merci"*. I don't know what he said but he certainly didn't tell me the time.

My teacher asked me: "What did he say?" I said he told me the time. So, she then enquired, *"Et donc quelle heure est-il?"*

I said, "I don't know. I didn't understand him". I didn't own a watch at that time.

She looked at her watch and said, *"Il est cinq heures et quart."* Which, of course, I then had to repeat.

Seeing the Eiffel Tower for the first time from the *Trocadéro* viewing area, that is what left the biggest impression on me; and travelling in the *métro* which was as good as a fairground ride. I wanted to come back to Paris and I wanted to try to learn French.

One-way French Exchange

I was 16 when I left home to visit a French family in Brive-la-Gaillarde. It was at the beginning of August 1970. This was only the second time I had been away from my parents; the first being on the school trip to Paris four years earlier. My French teacher had got in touch with an organisation in Angoulême whose abbreviated name was SILC (*Séjours Internationaux Linguistiques et Culturels*); and, if my memory serves me correctly, a Monsieur Deschamps wrote to my teacher with the details of the arrangements for my proposed *séjour*. I was to travel from Victoria Station with a French group returning to France. I was sent a cloth badge/*un écusson* with SILC written on it, and my mother duly sewed this on the front of my school blazer. On the day of reckoning, I was put on a train to London. I was wearing my school uniform and I had all my worldly possessions in my small suitcase which was not heavy or full. It contained some underwear and socks, a pair of jeans, a pair of white shorts and white plimsolls (basically my PE kit) and a few white shirts. In addition, I had some toothpaste and a toothbrush, a comb and a bottle of shampoo. I had some pocket money (*de l'argent de poche*) for emergencies. I took a notepad and pen, and a pocket-sized French dictionary. I had a one year temporary passport. My opening phrase was going to be: "*Bonjour, je suis content de vous voir*".

I found the group at Victoria Station. I was overdressed in comparison; and, of course, I was the only person sporting the *SILC écusson*. We took the train to Dover. I shared a carriage with four or five French boys and girls. One boy had his suitcase in front of him on the floor. It had a label with "*Trouvé*" written on it. I asked him in a mixture of English and French whether he had lost his suitcase? He looked puzzled. I pointed to the label "Found," I said. "*Trouvé* means found." I repeated. He said that Trouvé was his surname. I think his name was Jean Pierre Trouvé and he may have come from Rennes. We boarded a ferry to

Calais and then a train to Paris. In Paris, we were taken for dinner somewhere by coach, and then dropped off at various stations. I was travelling with three others from Gare d'Austerlitz to Brive, except the other three were leaving the train at Limoges and I was to travel on alone for about another hour. The main issue was that our train was delayed by nearly five hours. I was supposed to arrive just before midnight. The French public phone service was not good, but I still thought maybe someone would have telephoned the family to inform them of the delay. I slept most of the journey until the others left the train. I arrived in Brive station around 4.00 a.m. in the morning. I took the underpass and climbed the stairs following the *Sortie* signs. I was reciting in my head "*Bonjour*" or was it now, "*Bonsoir, je suis content de vous voir*", not really believing anyone would be there to meet me.

As I entered the station hall, I was pounced upon by a woman, shouting my name. I said, "Yes". She grabbed my suitcase, gave me a big hug, and whisked me off into her car. If I hadn't been so tired, I might have thought I was being kidnapped. She drove and talked in French, interspersed with my name.

In the space of three minutes, she had pronounced my name in more different ways than I thought possible: "Piterrr", "Peeeeterr", "Petterr", "Petter", and so forth, with such an impressive variety of intonations. I could sense I was in safe hands. I said a few things. We got to her house and I met her son. We stayed up for another two hours drinking fruit juice before I was shown my bed. They did most of the talking. I was bombarded with questions. I understood a few. I answered a few. The mother had been backwards and forwards to the station every hour since midnight. She had pounced on a few other boys who probably did think she was about to kidnap them.

A few hours later, about midday, we had breakfast of *tartines*, pieces of French bread with butter and jam *(confiture)*, and a bowl of milky coffee *(café au lait)*; and then we drove to Argentat where I was to stay for three weeks with the whole family. During that August, my French teacher and her husband, the maths teacher, called in to see me on their way to spend their summer holiday in Sarlat. You would have thought the Queen of England had arrived with Prince Philip. The French red carpet was rolled out. At lunch, my maths teacher was as quiet as me. But, when put on the spot, he produced his two words of French: *la bouffe* and *la boustifaille* (slang words for food – grub or nosh). The pronouncing of those two words by *le Prince Philip* were never forgotten by the family; and I added them to my French vocabulary.

To give you a flavour of that first trip to Brive, there were two early incidents that spring to mind. At my first breakfast in Argentat, I was looking forward to having "*tartines*" again and possibly *croissants*. I definitely liked French bread. We never had it in England at that time, well certainly not *chez nous*. I sat down at the kitchen table and the mother's face lit up. She couldn't stop smiling. "*Cornflake! Cornflake! Cornflake!*" she exclaimed ecstatically. And she went to the cupboard and produced a medium-sized box of Kellogg's Cornflakes. I tried my best to be excited, as she poured me a huge portion into a bowl and filled it up with milk. I was invited to sprinkle on some sugar cubes! She kept asking me, while I was trying to eat them: *"Les Cornflake sont-ils bons?"*

"Très bons," I said. *"Merci beaucoup pour les Cornflake."* They were *dégueulasses* – excuse my French. After a few mouthfuls, I thought I was going to be sick. Was it the Cornflakes or *le lait frais* (fresh milk). I struggled on. I finally finished the bowlful. I was not feeling good. I put on a brave face.

"Encore," she said. *"Encore. Vous ne les aimez pas?"* (All the rest of the family used *tu* when they spoke to me. She thought she had to wait a few days before asking my permission to address me using the familiar form *tu*. Later she told me that she knew a husband and wife couple who addressed each other all their lives using *vous*! I suspected it might have been her parents).

"Ils étaient très bons, merci; vraiment, merci pour les Cornflake; non, vraiment, j'en ai trop mangé déjà." I didn't want to upset her. My parents had told me to be on my best behaviour – and to remember my manners – at all times.

I had a stomach ache (*j'avais mal au ventre*) for most of the day. Although I never said anything, the mother sensed there was something wrong. Next day, I was given a choice of *tartines ou Cornflake*. I never did eat any more of those *Cornflake*. The mother didn't insist.

A full year or so later, she plucked up the courage to tell me that she had spent nearly a whole week searching the town shops in Brive and Argentat to try to find some *Cornflake*. She was beginning to despair. But then finally she went into yet another grocery store (*une épicérie*) which had one box left, or rather left over. The grocer (*l'épicier*) had told her that it was an old box, and it may have been in his storeroom for several years.

"*Les Cornflakes étaient mauvais! Mon pauvre Peeeterr!*" she exclaimed, and couldn't stop herself from laughing out loud. I said those *Cornflake* had nearly made me sick. And we both laughed our heads off.

Soon after I arrived, Philippe, the son, a few months older than me, declared that today we were going to *faire du bateau sur la Dordogne*, which he kindly translated into English as: "We are going to make the boat on the Dordogne".

The Dordogne was about a two hundred yard walk away at the bottom of the garden and through a field. I had no experience of boat building. At school, I had chosen metalwork instead of woodwork, and I was still struggling with bending a piece of metal over an anvil, while other boys were taking home coat hooks and pokers that they had made. Anyway, he explained to me that he would do the rowing, but I could try if I wanted to. Bearing in mind I couldn't swim (*je ne savais pas nager*) and I had a real fear of drowning, the last thing I wanted to do was to go out, into deep water, in a rowing boat with a boy I hardly knew. The mother insisted I wore a *gilet de sauvetage* (life-jacket). She did not have to insist. She had previously taken me into town to buy a pair of swimming shorts (*un maillot de bain*) as I had not brought a pair with me.The boat was tied to a tree, and we dragged it down to the river. The mother came to see the launch and then went back to the house to prepare lunch.

Philippe got in the boat and set up the oars (*les rames*). I sheepishly and clumsily got in the boat and sat down facing the oarsman. I asked him how deep the river was. Not as deep here as up there, he told me, and pointed behind him to where we were headed. It was a beautiful, sunny day. The water was calm. We were the only two on the river. Little did I know what was in store for me. After about half an hour or so, Philippe stopped rowing. He declared that we, I stress we, we were going to test the life-jacket. I was the only one wearing a life-jacket.

"Yes," he said, "you jump in the river."

"You must be joking," I said. "I can't swim. It's very deep".

He insisted. "We have to test the life-jacket."

I said, "If I jump in the river, I could drown."

He tried to reassure me that he would jump in and save me. I said under no circumstances was I going to jump. He was adamant. "*Dépêche-toi* ("Hurry up")," he said, "it's nearly lunchtime."

"*Impossible,*" I protested.

"*Impossible n'est pas français*" was one of his favourite ripostes (and apparently one of Napoleon's too).

It was decided, finally, after lengthy Anglo-French discussions, that I would stand at the other end of the boat, and he would push me in.

I stayed calm. I was going to die. He pushed me in. After the initial splash, my head remained above the water level surrounded by the life-jacket. It was as if I was somehow suspended from the sky, almost vertically. I did not move. All I could see was water. My whole life flashed before me: to that day I went to the dentist and passed out. I had been made to watch my brother scream in pain as he had a nerve extracted from his tooth. I had to go back the following week. We never went to the dentist together ever again; that day I scored a hat trick in a primary school football match against another school. I was accused of hogging the ball. I only touched it three times; that day I delivered a box of groceries, on my after-school grocery round, and got bitten by a vicious Alsation dog. The same dog had to be put down the following week after hurdling the garden fence and biting the first person it came across in the street; that day I dropped a catch in an important secondary school cricket match, the batsman had made 5 runs; he went on to make over 60 runs and their team over 100 runs. We went into bat and were all out for under 20 runs. I was blamed for dropping the catch; those disgusting toilets at the *Lycée St Louis* on the school trip to Paris; and the nasty toxic fumes from the dogfish tank in the biology lab at school. My short eventful life was coming to an end. I could envisage the headlines in the local paper: "Life-vest test goes wrong. Much loved son drowns in the Dordogne". Philippe is quoted as admitting to pushing me in, but "only because he would not jump."

I stayed still. I was very calm. I hadn't long left. I was defenceless. He had only to strike me over the head with one of the oars and I would be gone. The Dordogne shark would be along any minute to bite off both my legs. Philippe shouted at my head for me to move my arms and legs. I could only move my eyes.

I fixed them on him, trying to convey the message. "If I manage to get back in that boat, I am going to murder you."

He manoeuvred the boat alongside my head and asked me how I was feeling: "*Comment ça va?*"

"Not too bad," I said. I grabbed the side of the boat with both hands, and he hauled me back on board. The life-jacket had done its job.

A few days later we were back on the river. This time we headed the other way, towards the bridge at Argentat. I had a go at rowing. Our progress was slow. A storm (*un orage*) was brewing. The closer we got to the bridge, the darker it became. Then the heavens opened up: violent huge streaks of lightning (*la foudre*) directly overhead, accompanied by immediate explosions of thunder (*coups de tonnerre*) and a torrent of rain. Philippe steered the boat to the side of the river and told me to get out. I stepped out. The water was only about a foot deep. We dragged the boat onto the bank and left it. We walked and ran, as fast as we could, through a dense jungle of riverside flora, back towards our starting point. We were both in bare feet. There were no stinging nettles as such, but my feet stung (and so did his) every step of the way. The incredible firework display above us was unrelenting, as was the rain. We were soaked to the skin. About fifty yards from where we had left our footwear, we saw Philippe's mother decked out in wellington boots and holding a golfing umbrella. She waved to us and then, knowing we were safe, she turned and quickly set off back towards the house. We followed on just as quickly. I have never ever since experienced such a storm.

This is not the book to recount my life with this family. Since the age of 16, they have treated me like a family member, and as an English friend, and continue to do so. I am forever grateful for their kindness. Sadly, both parents have passed away; as have my own parents, my French teacher and her husband; and Windsor Davies too. I was thankful to be able to take my mother to meet the family in Argentat, and also to take her to *Le Gouffre de Padirac* and to *Rocamadour*, excursions to which I was taken by the family during that first trip.

Life-vest test

We did have swimming lessons at school. In PE we were taken, on several occasions, to the open-air swimming pool in the local park. I hated going. The water temperature was so cold, and it was no warmer outside of the pool. The boys who could already swim stayed at the deep end with the teacher who was obviously the one with potential to be an Olympic coach. They were diving off the diving boards and doing life-saving exercises. The rest of us, about 15 of us, went down the shallow end with the other, fully clothed teacher. The water was three feet deep, which was deep enough for me. It was freezing. No-one wanted to put his head under water or let go of the side or end of the pool, least of all me. Our teacher lay prostrate on a stool in front of us on dry land. We watched him demonstrate the breast stroke; moving his arms and legs simultaneously. If we hadn't been so cold, we might have found it funny to see him flapping about on a stool. One or two boys swore at him under their breath. He told us to back away about six feet from the end of the pool and to try to float back to the end. We had those white polystyrene floats to assist. Most of us hopped on one leg. We did this for the whole lesson. The boy, next to me, had told me that he could actually swim but because he didn't want to go in the deep end, he was pretending otherwise. This boy, after hopping with me for about the sixth or seventh time, floated majestically back to the end without the aid of the float. The teacher saw him and was ecstatic.

"He can swim! He can swim! He's learned to swim! Let that be encouragement to all of you!". It wasn't. None of us learned to swim.

When I was 35 years old, I went to a Swim School in Wales, owned by Jill and her partner Michael. It was a money-back guarantee weekend including board and lodging. The pool was heated. I had one-to-one lessons with Jill. By lunch-time on the first day I had learned to float and to do the breast stroke!

My return trip home from that first visit was an adventure. I had no-one from SILC to accompany me. Mother and son put me on the train from Brive to Paris. I don't know who was more relieved me or them, that I had survived their kindness and generosity and all their unconscious efforts to try to kill me. My suitcase was a lot heavier. I had bought a few chocolates and biscuits to take back as presents for my own family. My French family had presented me with not one, but with two large dictionaries: a Harrap's French-English dictionary and a Petit Larousse French dictionary, two bibles of the French language whose editions, though a bit battered through time and usage, and a little outdated, remain to this day the basis for increasing my knowledge of the French language and culture.

I had been drilled in the kitchen at Argentat for several days on how to navigate the *métro* in Paris. I followed the instructions given. On arrival at Gare d'Austerlitz, I followed the sign to the *métro*. I bought *un ticket* at *le guichet*. The tickets were all one price no matter the length of the journey. I followed the sign for *Ligne 5 (M5)* and *direction: Eglise de Pantin* (which at that time was the end of the line). I took the train and got out at *la station République* and looked for the sign *Correspondance* and then followed the sign for *Ligne 3 (M3) direction: Gare St. Lazare* and boarded the train. It went to plan.

My rail and boat ticket was an open return from my home town to Brive. I had arranged this through a local travel agent. I boarded the boat train at Gare St. Lazare, having had my ticket punched by *le poinçonneur/le contrôleur* on entry to the platform. Nowadays, *poinçonneurs* have largely been replaced by *compostage* machines where you have to date and validate your own ticket. I cannot remember any more about that first solo return journey. However, as much as I liked being in France, I was happy to be back in England again.

Philippe, his wife and two children came to visit me in 1994. They arrived the very weekend that I was playing in the final of a doubles tennis tournament at Crawley Tennis Club. They were obliged to come to watch me play. I had been paired at random with another club player whose name was Peter Death. Death was a good player and he instructed me clearly in our preliminary matches. When serving, I was to serve the ball in, and then keep out of the way and let him play the point. When receiving service, I was to return the ball and get it in court, and then keep out of the way while he played the point. This approach worked well. Our opponents tried of course to target me. But Death was all over the court intercepting at the net, retrieving balls from the base-line, lobbing and smashing. You could not ask for a better Death. We reached the final. Our opponents thought that I could barely hit the ball, such was the protection that Death was giving me. More often than not, they left the court wide open, and I hit a few winners to complement those of Death. He warned me not to get overconfident. He reminded me that my role was just to return the ball and then get out of the way. We won the final against the odds. Death did not attempt to hurdle the net, and nor did I; at school, in the high jump, I had barely cleared two feet six inches. P.Death and P.Voice are proudly displayed on the Honours Board (*le palmarès*) at the Club, as winners of the 1994 Mens Doubles Tournament.

I returned home that day, triumphant, with Philippe and his family, and we went to collect my mother for lunch. Philippe announced to her: "*Peter is a winer!*" My mother suspected that I was a winner. But she never let me forget that Philippe had announced that I was a "*winer*".

The "Winers"

Part 5

A Sampling of French Grammar

L'Orthographe (Spelling)

If you know your French onions, the spelling is **les oignons;** or, if you wish, **les ognons,** following the recommended Spelling Rectifications of 1990 of the *Académie française* (**AFSR 1990**).

Other gems:
L'év**é**nement may now be spelled l'év**è**nement.
La cha**î**ne → la cha**i**ne
Le co**û**t → le co**u**t
Le porte-monnaie → le portemonnaie
Une sage-femme → une sagefemme (midwife)

Cent vingt six → cent-vingt-six (126)

Le joaill**i**er → le joailler (jeweller)
Le quincaill**i**er → le quincailler (the iron monger)

Le or La? C'est la question!

We all know that French nouns are either masculine or feminine. What we don't know is which ones are which. We don't have this problem in English.

It's **la** moustache, **la** barbe (beard), **le** soutien-gorge (bra), **les** collants (tights).

There seems to be no rhyme nor reason. You must learn the gender/article (*le* or *la*) along with the noun.

There are a few helpful tips, for example:

Nouns ending in *-tion* are 99.9% feminine: eg. *la natation, la station, la vaccination, la fabrication, la cohabitation* etc. The only exceptions I know are *le bastion* and *le cation.*

Nouns ending in *-ette* are 99.9% feminine: eg. *une omelette, une galette* etc. The one exception I know is *le squelette.*

Nouns ending in **-eau** are 99.9% masculine: eg. *le poireau, le rideau, le seau, le plateau* etc. Two exceptions: *de l'eau* (water) and *la peau* (skin).

But then you get words ending in *– ée* that definitely look feminine, and some are, and some are not:

le musée, le trophée, le lycée, le scarabée (beetle),
la fusée, l'armée, la fée, une idée, la mosquée, une araignée (spider).

Incidentally, the *Académie française* has advised that it should be <u>**la**</u> *Covid-19* and <u>not</u> *le Covid-19.* In the written language, from what I have seen, the feminine form is being adhered to; but in conversation, people switch between *le* and *la*, and the *le* form seems to roll off the tongue more easily. See Appendix 11 for some Coronavirus vocabulary.

Some nouns have both genders and change meaning

A few examples:

Le Tour de France and *La Tour Eiffel.*
Le livre (book); *La livre sterling* (£).
Le pâté; *La pâtée* (dog food).
Le manche (handle); *La manche* (sleeve);
La Manche (English Channel).
Le voile (veil); *La voile* (sail, sailing).

When it comes to people and professions most nouns have both a masculine and feminine form:

For example, l'acteur/l'actrice; l'infirmier/l'infirmière (nurses); les soignants/ les soignantes (carers); le lecteur/la lectrice (reader); le téléspectateur/la téléspectatrice (viewer); l'auditeur/l'auditrice (listener); un influenceur/une influenceuse; un avocat/une avocate(barrister); un policier/une policière.

In the case of what French linguists call *les mots épicènes* (words of one gender applying to both sexes) a feminine form has been created for many such nouns. *Un enfant* and *une enfant* is not incorrect.

It was usual, in the now distant past, for example, to refer to a female Government Minister as *Madame le Ministre*. Similarly, a female *professeur* (secondary school teacher) would be referred to as *une femme professeur*.

In recent times, there has been a desire or pressure to use appropriate female forms of such nouns. So now we have:

Le ministre/la ministre; le député/la députée (MP); le maire/la maire; le président/la présidente (chairman/woman); un auteur/une auteure; un écrivain/une écrivaine; le professeur/la professeure; le/la porte-parole (spokesperson); le préfet/la préfète.

There are some *mots épicènes* whose feminisation is not obvious to me. For example: *un médecin* refers still to both a male and female doctor; you can say *une femme médecin*. *Le mannequin* (catwalk model) does not have a feminine form although most of them are women.

For animals, you can say, for example, *un tigre mâle* and *un tigre femelle*. But there are of course female forms for some animals: *un bouc/une chèvre, un chien/une chienne, un cheval/une jument, un jars/une oie, un lièvre/une hase, etc.*

Not all *mots épicènes* are of masculine gender; there are fewer feminine nouns common to both sexes, of note are*:*

Brute (bully), *bête, vedette, star, victime, idole.*

Une sage-femme is a midwife, and the majority are women. The *Académie française* decided that the term should apply to both sexes. After all, *un homme sage-femme* would sound a little odd.

According to one source[5], a term is available to describe male mid-wives since the 1980s: *un maïeuticien*.

Another recent trend, in the current climate in which women are increasingly more assertive in striving for equality, is a sensitivity on the part of TV presenters to consider making a distinction between men and women, and not to lump them together.

When referring to two or more persons of each gender in French, the masculine form of the noun has always taken precedence: *eg. Chers Lecteurs,* Dear Readers *(*where *lecteurs* covers both male and female readers).

In English, if we refer to nurses and carers, we mean both male and female staff; the majority we assume are female and we would designate male nurses only if there was a specific need to identify that group or an individual. If the French refer to *les infirmiers* and *les soignants*, they are also referring to both male and female staff. But since there are words in French for female nurses and carers, and the latter are in the majority, why should the female form not take precedence, and nurses and carers be referred to as *les infirmières* and *les soignantes*.

To be politically correct, should TV presenters refer now specifically to both their *téléspectateurs* and *téléspectatrices;* and when saying good night should they not say *bonsoir à tous et à toutes?*

The debate continues. What is worse, and *très compliqué,* is if this spreads to the written language, so called *l'écriture inclusive,* for example:

Cher(s) étudiant(s) et Chère(s) étudiante(s), instead of just *Chers étudiants.*

---

5 "Le français correct pour les Nuls" by Jean-Joseph Julard.

La Ponctuation

A full-stop is *un point* and a comma is *une virgule*.
1.5 one <u>point</u> five in French is *un <u>virgule</u> cinq*: 1,5; and 9.6 is *neuf virgule six*: 9,6.
2,600 two thousand six hundred is *deux <u>mille</u> six <u>cents</u>*: 2.600.
2,600,000 two million six hundred thousand is *deux millions six <u>cent</u> mille*: 2.600.000.
Vendez votre voiture.fr (vendez votre voiture <u>point</u> fr) is the equivalent of We Buy any Car.com (we buy any car <u>dot</u> com).

Entre crochets: [between square brackets].
Entre paranthèses: (between round brackets).
Entre guillemets: "in inverted commas".
<u>*Les chiffres/les numéraux/les nombres*</u>
Les chiffres romains:
MDCLXVI = 1666
1666 mil six cent soixante six 2021 l'an deux mil vingt et un (mil =mille = a thousand in referring to specific years*).
Note*: six cent<u>s</u> (600)* <u>but</u> *six cent cinq (605) (cent* is invariable if followed by another number).
Note: quatre-vinqt<u>s</u> (80) <u>but</u> tournez à la page quatre-vingt (80), quatre-vinqt-un (81), trente-<u>et</u>-un (31), quarante-<u>et</u>-un (41).
Note: *six mille (6.000) (mille 1.000* is always invariable);
[six mille<u>s</u> usually means *6 nautical miles* ie. *six noeuds* (knots) (1852 *mètres* is 1 nautical mile)].

Un million is 1.000.000 *(mille mille)*; *un milliard* is 1,000,000,000 *(mille millions)* and *un billion* is 1,000,000,000,000 *(un million des millions)*.

Le trait d'union (the hyphen)

The 1990 Spelling Recommendations of the *Académie française*
(**AFSR1990**) state that:

for numbers above 100, the hyphen may now also be used; whereas
previously the hyphen was correctly used only in numbers below
100.

e.g., 22 *vingt-deux;* 45 *quarante-cinq;*

106 *cent six* **or** *cent-six;*

5.308 *cinq mille trois cent huit* **or**

cinq-mille-trois-cent-huit.

For certain common hyphenated words, the hyphen may be
replaced by joining the words together. This also simplifies the
plural of such words:

e.g., *Le weekend* (for *le week-end*); *le fairplay* (for *le fair-play*) and
similarly *le croquemonsieur, le portemonnaie, la sagefemme, le tirebouchon,
le mangetout* etc.

All of which +s in the plural: eg. *les weekends.*

L'apostrophe

J'aime la bière. C'est la vie. L'hexagone. L'oeuvre d'art.

The French do not suffer from the grocer's apostrophe syndrome
which consists in putting the apostrophe in the wrong place or
adding one when none is needed. However, I know of three
examples where there is an apostrophe followed by s ('s) in French:
Fouquet's and *Maxim's* both famous establishments in Paris.

The only noun I know is *le pin's* and its plural form *les pin's,* which
are lapel or pin badges.

In all three examples the *s* and the *preceding consonant* are pronounced.
The verb *apostropher qqn.* means to speak to someone abruptly
sans politesse.

Les Accents

There are so many different accents:
le circonflexe (for example fête, bête, traître, bâtiment), **la cédille** (for example français, leçon, garçon), **le tréma** (for example Noël, cocaïne, héroïne), **l'accent grave** (for example pièce, voilà, où), **l'accent aigu** (for example chérie, véritable, événement, mangé).

Le circonflexe

I wonder how the French know when to add a circumflex and when not to do so. It may be down to subtleties in pronunciation which may or may not still be made by people in different regions and of different generations; or, in some cases, to compensate for a letter "s" no longer retained. In a few cases, it helps to distinguish the meaning of words otherwise spelt the same. Perhaps, like me, the French need to consult a dictionary quite frequently.

La tâche (*tarsh*) task; *la tache* (*tash*) stain.

Les pâtes (*part*) pasta; *la patte* (*pat*) paw.

Le château, le gâteau but: *le bateau, le chapeau, le plateau* (tray; media platform/panel; plateau), *le tableau, le drapeau.*

La fête, la bête, le hêtre (beech tree), *le chêne* (oak tree), *le frêne* (ash tree), *une guêpe* <u>but</u>: *Sète, un guépard.*

L'hôte, l'hôtel, <u>but</u> *l'otage; le pôle,* <u>but</u> *la métropole, le monopole.*

La côte/la cote; la zone, le clone, l'aumône, le dôme, un atome, un monôme.

La bûche, jeûner, <u>but</u> *la ruche, le déjeuner.*

Le vôtre/votre, la voûte/la route/le doute/le coût/le bout.

L'abîme, le dîner, <u>but</u> *la cime, décliner.*

La chaîne <u>but</u> *la haine.*

The **AFSR1990** recommends that since the circumflex over the *û* and the *î* does not make any difference to pronunciation, it can be eliminated. However, the circumflex needs to be maintained on a few words where it indicates a difference of meaning: *mûr/mur, jeûne/jeune, sûr/sur, dû/du*; and in the spelling of proper names: e.g., *Nîmes*, **nîmois**.

La cédille

The cedilla is placed exclusively under the letter *c* to soften it: *e.g., les Français; recevoir* but *j'ai reçu; décevoir* but *je suis déçu (I am disappointed); le reçu* but *le recepissé (receipt); la leçon* but *le lycée.*

Le tréma

The *tréma* (diaresis) is <u>two dots</u> placed horizontally above the vowels e, i and u, to indicate that the preceding vowel has to be pronounced separately:
e.g., naïf (<u>but</u> le lait), faïence, canoë.

The **AFSR1990** points to certain words that cause difficulties in pronunciation because the two dots have been misplaced above a mute vowel. It recommends therefore correcting this anomaly, in such words as: *aiguë* to *aigüe*; *ambiguë* to *ambigüe*, *ambiguïté* to *ambigüité*, *contiguë* to *contigüe*, *exiguë* to *exigüe*, *ciguë* to *cigüe* (hemlock). It suggests adding the diaresis to a few other words to aid pronunciation: e.g., *gageure* to *gageüre*, *rongeure* to *rongeüre*, *mangeure* to **mangeüre**, *vergeure* to *vergeüre*, and the verb *arguer* (to argue) to *argüer* (and all forms of its conjugation).

Lettre majuscule ou lettre minuscule?

(Capital letter or small letter)

*Le français (*French language*); la langue française* but *le(s) Français (French man/men/people); la(les) Française(s) (Frenchwoman/women).*
Similarly with other languages and nationalities *(l'anglais, English (language); les Anglais, the English etc.).*
Les mois de l'année: janvier, février, mars etc.
Les saisons: l'hiver, le printemps, l'automne, l'été.

I am/it is

It is hot/cold

<u>The weather</u>
Il <u>fait</u> du soleil; <u>il fait</u> du vent, <u>il fait</u> un beau temps, il <u>fait froid</u>; il <u>fait</u> chaud.
It is sunny; it is windy; it's fine weather; it's cold; it's hot.
<u>Milk, soup, coffee, etc.</u>
Le lait <u>est</u> froid. Mon café <u>n'est</u> pas chaud. Ma soupe <u>est</u> froide (ma soupe -elle- ma soupe: elle est froide).

To tell the time
<u>Il est</u> *cinq heures.*
<u>Il est</u> *minuit.*
<u>Il est</u> *deux heures moins le quart.*
<u>Il est</u> *six heures et demie.*

Someone is hot/cold

<u>J'ai</u> chaud / <u>J'ai</u> froid: I am hot / I am cold.
Elle <u>a</u> chaud / Elle <u>a</u> froid: She is hot / she is cold.
NB: Do <u>not</u> say when referring to a female person *"Elle <u>est</u> chaude"* (this means: *"she is "sexy" hot"*); similarly, *"Elle <u>est</u> froide"* (could mean: *"she is frigid"*).
Similarly, use the verb <u>*avoir*</u> to say:
<u>J'ai</u> vingt cinq ans: I am 25 years old.
<u>J'ai</u> peur: I am afraid.
<u>J'ai</u> tort / raison: I am wrong / right.
<u>J'ai</u> sommeil: I am sleepy.
<u>J'ai</u> faim / soif: I am hungry / thirsty.

Si nous + imperfect tense?

Suppose we do something?
Si nous allions au cinéma? Shall we go to the cinema?
Si nous allions au lit?
Si nous faisions une tasse de thé?
Si nous prenions le train (au lieu d'y aller en voiture)?

La Prononciation

First there may be some difficulties in pronunciation because your mother tongue is English:

The French r sound from the back of the throat; the French u sound (like oo preceded by trying to say ee); and the French nasal vowels, so called because they are produced with a bit of air from the nose; as opposed to oral vowels which are not.

Try pronouncing the following:

La *grenouille, rural, un rhume (a cold), route, rouge, le riz (rice)*.

(Rhume – pronounced something like Inspector Clusoe (Peter Sellers) in the film The Pink Panther: *"I'd like a Rrrooom"*, but with the eeoo (u) vowel sound).

Beaucoup/beau cul! (coo/ceeoo).

Une boule de neige (snowball)/*une bulle de neige* (snow bubble (globe) souvenir).

Le corps? Il court encore.

Henriette Walter, in her excellent book "*Le français dans tous les sens*", identifies 4 nasal vowel sounds as in:

Un/grand/pain/rond

Un/pain –a distinction between these two nasal vowel sounds, she notes (in 1986), is disappearing in the Paris region; and possibly more widely among the younger population too. Henriette Walter observes no distinction between *brun* and *brin;* and *un* tolérant and *intolérant.*

With regard to oral vowel sounds, she notes a tendency for a distinction not to be made between the longer and shorter sounds in:

Pâte (pronounced like English part) – *Patte* (pat)

Maître – Mètre

Fête – Faites

With the shorter vowel sound adopted for both.

I always noted my French teacher's pronunciation of *la tâche* (tarsh) task; and *la tache* (tash) stain.

The verbs are *tâcher* (to try) and *tacher* (to stain). But this was 50 years ago! I have recently (12 March 2021) heard Eric Zemmour on C News say "*la séparation des tâches*" – pronounced more like *tash* and not *tarsh*- therefore making little or no distinction between *tâches* and *taches* in pronunciation.

In the **AFSR1990**, the *Académie* acknowledges that there is no difference in pronunciation of the vowel sound in *le château* and *le bateau*, but there may still be a distinction in tonality between other vowel sounds, such as *le nôtre* and *notre*; *la côte/la cote*; or *(le) pôle* and *(la) métropole*.

Other words to note:

Un os (oss); des os (o) bones.

Un oeuf (erf); des oeufs (zeux) eggs.

Un boeuf (berf); des boeufs (beux).

*Du poisson (*some fish; pronounced pwa<u>ss</u>on*); du poison (*poison; pronounced pwa<u>z</u>on*).*

*Des chev<u>eux</u> (*hair*); des chev<u>aux</u> (*horses*).*

*Un canard (*a duck*); un connard (*a jerk, idiot*).*

Femme (like <u>fam</u> in family*); faim (*like French *fin* / rhyming with *vin*).

La pôele (pwal – frying pan*); le poil (pwal* -animal hair*); la moelle (mwal* -bone marrow*).*

(<u>Le</u> pôele is a stove*; le four* oven*; une cuisinière à gaz* gas cooker*).*

(À poil means naked*; anglais jusqu'à la moelle des os (*English to the bone*); corrompu jusqu'à la moelle (rotten to the core)).*

Un million; un milliard (the *illi* sound is pronounced like in English).

Le village (vee <u>lar</u> je).

Une <u>anguille</u> (an eel) *on <u>gee</u> j* (g as in geese; j like y(er)); but *une <u>aiguille</u>* (a needle) *ay <u>gwee</u>j* (ay as in hay; gwee y(er)).

(Similarly *les aiguilleurs* – railway points and pointsmen; *les aiguilleurs du ciel* air traffic controllers).

There are difficulties in pronunciation, where French words or French word-endings have the same spelling but are pronounced differently:

ending	pronounced	examples	pronounced	examples
-il	like English ee	gentil, fusil, outil	like English eel	cil, exil, fil, péril, subtil
-ille	ee y(er)	fille, sillage, la Bastille, pillage	eel	ville, tranquille
-baye	bay	abbaye	by	cobaye, Bayeux
-ils	eel	les fils du coton	eess like beas(t)	le fils (son of family)
-et	ay as in hay	carnet, robinet, volet, jet	et as in bet	net; (tennis) set
-er	ay as in hay	défier, ramer, aimer, re-porter (to postpone) conseiller (to advise) conseiller (adviser)	er like English air	fier, amer, reporter (news reporter) supporter (football fan)

Some French words are difficult to understand or spell because they sound the same or their vowel sounds rhyme with other words:
Fois, foi, foie, foi(re), Foix; vert, vers, ver.
Quand, camp, con, Caen; près, pré, prêt.
Mal, mâle, malle; saint, sein, sain.
Peint, pain; temps, vent, tant, gens.
Pot, peau, Pau.
Salle, poisson, lycée, inertie, citoyen (all have the same s sound).

In **AFSR1990**, the *Académie* recommends that, since it is not pronounced, the letter (i) may be eliminated in the spelling of:
le quincaill(i)er ironmonger (like English: cank eye yay);
la serpill(i)ère floor cloth (like: sair pea yair)
and *le joaill(i)er* jeweller.

All the preceding examples have been adapted or taken from the table on page 26 of Henriette Walter's book "*Le français dans tous les sens*".
Lastly, she notes that the **e** may be silent in:
Melon/tenir/venir (m'lon/t'nir/v'nir).
But not, for example, in:
dehors (outside), *frelon* (hornet).

At the airport bag check-in:
Enr(e)gistrement des Bagages,
the second e is silent, and the correct pronunciation is *l'engistrement.*
Note also: *La réouverture des boîtes de nuit* (the re-opening of night-clubs),
but: *rouvrir* is the verb to reopen.

H muet and h aspiré

What is the connection in French between the <u>owl</u>, the <u>hedgehog</u> and the <u>lobster</u>?

To hear a French person, speak English, you would think that there was no letter h at all in the French language.

French native speakers say more easily *"appy Birthday"* and *"ow can I elp you"*. To produce our h sound, they have to make a huge effort, leaving them out of breath to continue the conversation.

In English, we have a number of words beginning with a silent h: for example *heir, honest, honour* and *hour*.

Other words such as *hospital, house, head, horse, hungry, hand, happy* etc. are pronounced with an h.

There are in fact two types of h in the French language*: h muet* (silent h) and *h aspiré (aspirate h).* <u>Neither is pronounced</u>; <u>but there is an important distinction between the two.</u>

<u>For French words beginning with a silent h such as *homme,***there is a regular elision with the definite article:**
*L'h*omme, *l'h*ûitre, *l'h*exagone etc.
And **in the plural form the liaison is made between the definite article and the noun:**
Les <z> hommes, les <z> hûitres, les<z>hexagones.

<u>For French words beginning with an *h aspiré* such as *haricot, hanche, halle etc.* **there is no elision with the definite article:**
Le haricot, la hanche, le haut, la halle, le hanneton;
And **in the plural there is no liaison:**
Les haricots, les hanches, les hauts, les halles, les hannetons.
In both the singular and the plural, therefore, **the article (le, la or les) and the noun are pronounced separately.**

Au lieu d'hiberner, j'aimerais mieux hiverner
Sur la côte d'Azur!

Le hérisson

The larger French/English dictionaries put an asterisk ★ by words beginning with a *French h aspiré*; another reason to buy a good quality French/English dictionary. Henriette Walter in her excellent book "*Le français dans tous les sens*" p56-58 gives an historical explanation for the existence of the two different types of letter h. **Le hibou** (the owl), **le hérisson** (the hedgehog) and **le homard** (the lobster) all begin with the French letter *h aspiré*.

PART 6

Administrative Organisation of France

L'Aménagement du Territoire

Mainland France is nicknamed *l'Hexagone* as it has six sides; and is referred to as *la France métropolitaine* including, of course, *(l'île de) la Corse (Corsica),* birthplace of Napoleon Bonaparte. France also has overseas territories and regions.

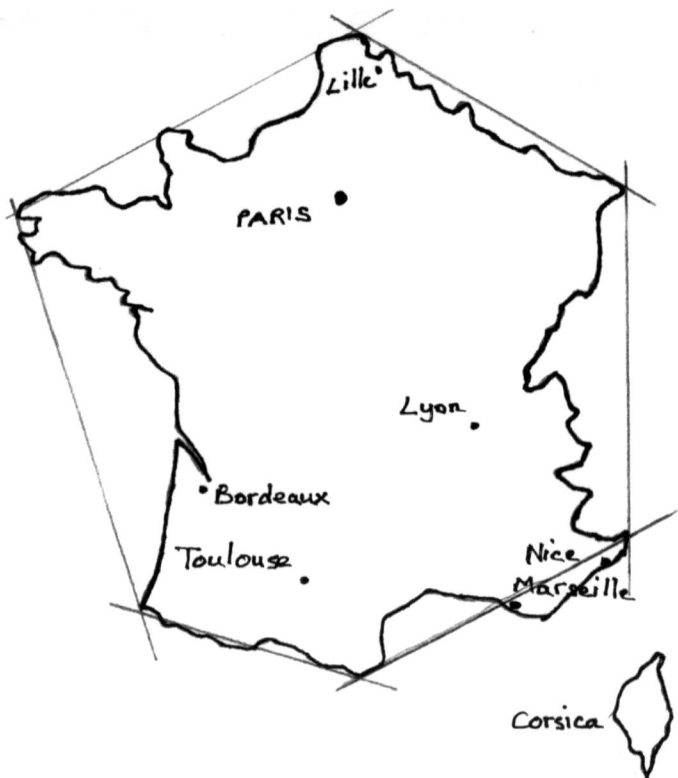

L'Hexagone

*La France métropolitaine (*including *la Corse) is currently divided into 13 régions.* Each region is made up of several *départements* of which there are 96. In addition, there are five overseas regions which are also departments. Each department is further divided into *communes* (municipalities) of which there are over 36,000. Municipalities are formed from *cantons* (approximately 2000) which are groupings of *arrondissements* (approximately 320), neither of which is a public or legal entity. Three urban communes (*Paris, Marseille* and *Lyon*) are divided into municipal arrondissements.

La France métropolitaine
22 regions prior to 2016; reorganised into 13 regions,
including Corsica.

There are a variety of local authorities at regional, departmental and municipal level:

Le conseil régional; le conseil départemental; et le conseil municipal.

At each level, councillors (*les conseillers/conseillères*) are elected for a six-year term by direct election, and it is they who in turn elect the President of the Regional Council, the President of the Department Council and the local Mayor.

The representative of the state in the *département* is *le préfet/la préfète*. His or her office is called *la Préfecture*. The prefect of the department containing the *chef-lieu de région* (main city or town of the region) is also the *préfet/préfète de région (regional prefect). Les sous-préfets* (sub-prefects) are responsible for the sub-divisions of departments. The office of a *sous-préfet* is based in another town or city known as *la Sous-Préfecture.*

Each *commune* has *une mairie* (town hall) and *un/une maire* (mayor).

Paris is divided into 20 *arrondissements*. Each *arrondissement* has *une mairie*. The Mayor of Paris is currently Anne Hidalgo. Her offices and staff are in the magnificent *Hôtel de Ville* near to Notre-Dame. She is the chief executive of Paris and is responsible for the administration and management of the city. She submits proposals and recommendations to the *Conseil de Paris* (Council of Paris) whose meetings she chairs as its *présidente*, as is the case of a *maire* in any other *commune* in France. The Council of Paris possesses simultaneously the powers of a municipal council (*conseil municipal*) and those of a departmental council (*conseil départemental*) for the *département de Paris (75)*. Paris is the only territorial collectivity in France to be both a *commune* and a *département*. The four *arrondissements* (1st, 2nd, 3rd and 4th) which make up the centre of the city have been grouped together since 2016 to make all the *arrondissements* more equal in terms of the size of population they serve. These four *arrondissements* are now known as *Paris Centre*. The *mairie* in the 3rd *arrondissement* was chosen to represent the new grouping, thus reducing the overall number of *maires* in Paris to 17. The postcodes for all

the 20 *arrondissements* have, however, been maintained.
Anne Hidalgo, a socialist, was re-elected as *Maire de Paris* in 2020
for a further term of six years.

Paris les 20 Arrondissements

1er	I	Louvre
2e	II	Bourse
3e	III	Temple
4e	IV	Hôtel de Ville
5e	V	Panthéon
6e	VI	Luxembourg
7e	VII	Palais Bourbon
8e	VIII	L'élysée
9e	IX	L'Opéra
10e	X	L'Entrepôt
11e	XI	Popincourt
12e	XII	Reuilly
13e	XIII	Gobelins
14e	XIV	Observatoire
15e	XV	Vaugirard
16e	XVI	Passy
17e	XVII	Batignolles–Monceau
18e	XVIII	Butte–Montmartre
19e	XIX	Buttes–Chaumont
20e	XX	Ménilmontant

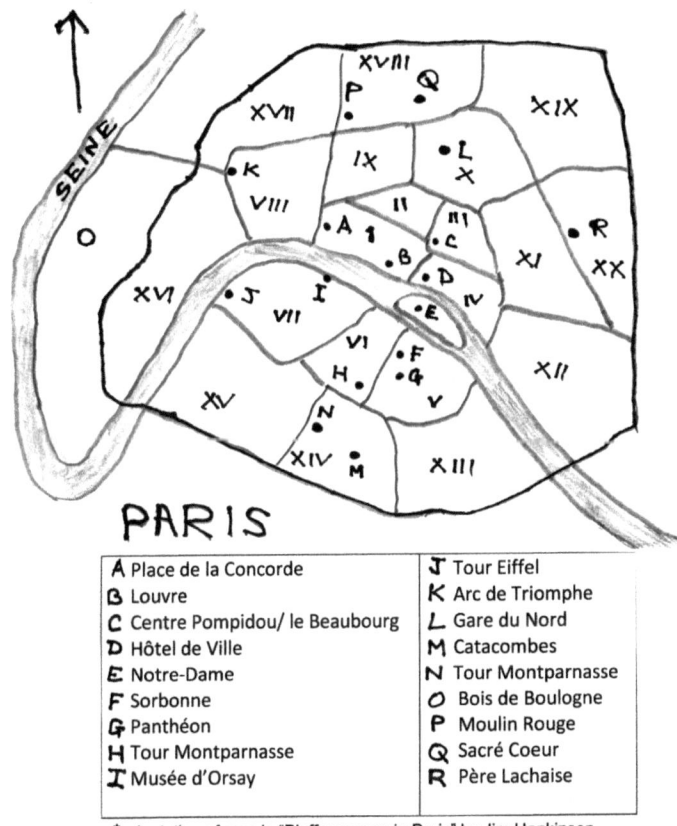

PARIS

A Place de la Concorde	**J** Tour Eiffel
B Louvre	**K** Arc de Triomphe
C Centre Pompidou/ le Beaubourg	**L** Gare du Nord
D Hôtel de Ville	**M** Catacombes
E Notre-Dame	**N** Tour Montparnasse
F Sorbonne	**O** Bois de Boulogne
G Panthéon	**P** Moulin Rouge
H Tour Montparnasse	**Q** Sacré Coeur
I Musée d'Orsay	**R** Père Lachaise

*adaptation of map in "Bluff your way in Paris" by Jim Hankinson

Le département de Paris est le № 75.

Valérie Pécresse is the current President of the Paris region (*Île-de-France*). She was elected as a regional councillor in December 2015 and was subsequently elected as the region's president (presiding officer). She is a member of the political grouping *libres, républicains, indépendants.*

She graduated both from HEC (*École des Hautes Études Commerciales*) and ENA (*École Nationale d'Administration*). She was a judge at the *Conseil d'État*, the highest administrative jurisdiction. She was advisor to President Jacques Chirac on new technologies and the internet. Elected an MP in 2002 and re-elected in 2007 and 2012, she was Minister for Higher Education and Research under President Nicolas Sarkozy. In 2011, she was appointed Budget Minister and government spokesperson. From June 2012 to December 2015, she acted as an MP, member of the Finance committee, and leader of the opposition at the *conseil régional* of the Paris region. In November 2015, she resigned from the Conseil d'État to focus on the Paris region.

French Regions and Departments

French Regions and Departments

Région: Auvergne-Rhône-Alpes	Région: Bourgogne-Franche-Comté	Région: Bretagne
Départements	Départements	Départements
03 Alllier	21 Côte-d'Or	22 Côtes-d'Armor
15 Cantal	58 Nièvre	29 Finistère
43 Haute-Loire	71 Saône-et-Loire	35 Ille-et-Vilaine
63 Puy-de Dôme	89 Yonne	56 Morbihan
01 Ain	25 Doubs	
07 Ardèche	39 Jura	
26 Drôme	70 Haute Saône	
38 Isère	90 Territoire de Belfort	
42 Loire		
69 Rhône		
73 Savoie		
74 Haute-Savoie		
Région: Centre-Val de Loire	Région: Pays de la Loire	Région: Corse[6]
Départements	Départements	Départements
18 Cher	44 Loire-Atlantique	2A Corse-du-Sud
28 Eure-et-Loir	49 Maine-et-Loire	2B Haute-Corse
36 Indre	53 Mayenne	
37 Indre-et-Loire	72 Sarthe	
41 Loir-et-Cher	85 Vendée	
45 Loiret		

---

6 Since Ist January 2018 Corsica is a single territorial collectivity.

Région: Grand Est	Région: Hauts-de-France	Région: Île-de-France (Paris region)
Départements	Départements	Départements
67 Bas-Rhin	59 Nord	75 Paris
68 Haut-Rhin	62 Pas-de-Calais	77 Seine-et-Marne
54 Meurthe-et-Moselle	02 Aisne	78 Yvelines
55 Meuse	60 Oise	91 Essonne
57 Moselle	80 Somme	92 Hauts-de-Seine
88 Vosges		93 Seine-St-Denis
08 Ardennes		94 Val-de-Marne
10 Aube		95 Val-D'Oise
51 Marne		
52 Haute-Marne		

Région: Normandie	Région: Nouvelle-Aquitaine	Région: Occitanie
Départements 27 Eure 76 Seine-Maritime 14 Calvados 50 Manche 61 Orne	Départements 16 Charente 17 Charente-Maritime 79 Deux-Sèvres 86 Vienne 24 Dordogne 33 Gironde 40 Landes 47 Lot-et-Garonne 64 Pyrénées-Atlantiques 19 Corrèze 23 Creuset 87 Haute-Vienne	Départements 01 Aude 30 Gard 34 Hérault 48 Lozère 66 Pyrénées-Orientales 09 Ariège 12 Aveyron 31 Haute-Garonne 32 Gers 46 Lot 65 Hautes-Pyrénées 81 Tarn 82 Tarn-et-Garonne
Région: Provence-Alpes-Côte d'Azur (PACA) Départements 04 Alpes-de-Haute-Provence 05 Hautes-Alpes 06 Alpes-Maritimes 13 Bouches-du-Rhône 83 Var 84 Vaucluse		

The number of each *département* is alphabetical in most cases. Until 2009, these numbers appeared as the last two numbers on French car number plates *(les plaques d'immatriculation/les plaques minéralogiques)*.[7] Since then, new car registrations do not bear the departmental number. However, a sticker with the number of the *département* can be added by the car owner, if they live there or not.

Paris registered plate pre 2009:

Since 2009, the format is as shown below, with 00 being the place holder for a sticker and a space for a regional logo above it.

7 The latter makes reference to the national mining administration which was responsible for issuing the plates in the early 20th century.

Des Bretons se baladent en Provence

The five overseas regions which are also departments are:

> Les Départements/Régions d'Outre-Mer (les DROM)
>
> 971 Guadeloupe
> 972 Martinique
> 973 Guyane
> 974 La Réunion
> 976 Mayotte

France also possesses overseas collectivities and territories.

> Les Collectivités (COM) et Les Territoires d'Outre-Mer (TOM)
> 984 Terres Australes et Antarctiques
> 986 Wallis et Futuna
> 987 Polynésie Française (of which Tahiti is the
> most populous island)
> 988 Nouvelle-Calédonie
> 975 Département de Saint-Pierre-et-Miquelon

France is a republic, and its head of state is the president who is elected for a term of five years. The current French President (*le Président*) is *Emmanuel Macron*. The French government is headed by a prime minister, appointed by the president, along with ministers appointed by the president on the initiative of the prime minister. The current Prime Minister (*le Premier ministre*) is *Jean Castex*.

The French parliament (*le parlement*) draws up and passes laws, and holds the government to account. It is made up of two chambers: *l'Assemblée Nationale (National Assembly)* which is composed of 577 *députés* (MPs) elected for a *mandat de cinq ans* (a term of five years) by direct election (*les élections législatives*); and *le Sénat* which is composed of 343 *sénateurs* (senators/peers) elected for a six-year term via an indirect election. The seat (*le siège*) of the National Assembly is *le Palais Bourbon*; and of the Senate is *le Palais du*

Luxembourg. Faire la navette entre les deux chambres refers to a draft bill (*un projet de loi*) which shuttles/goes to and fro between the two chambers (*une navette de bus* is a shuttle bus and *une navette spatiale* is a space shuttle). *La navette parlementaire* continues until one of the two chambers adopts, without modifying them, the texts presented by the other. When agreement cannot be reached between the two chambers, the decision of the National Assembly is final.

In the run-up to the French presidential elections in April 2022, you should be aware of the main political parties and their leaders:

Mainstream Right:
Les Républicains (LR)
Leader: Christian Jacob

Far Right
Le Rassemblement National (RN)
Leader: Marine Le Pen/Jordan Bardella

Centre
La République en Marche (LREM)
Leader: Emmanuel Macron

Centre Left
Le Parti Socialiste (PS)
Leader: Olivier Faure

Europe Écologie Les Verts (EELV) Green Party
Leader: Julien Bayou

Far Left
La France Insoumise (FI)
Leader: Jean-Luc Mélenchon

In the French regional elections on 20 and 27 June 2021, the turnout was very low. Two out of three voters did not bother to vote (*le taux d'abstention au second tour était de 65%*). Valérie Pécresse (LR) was re-elected as President of the Île-de-France region. Xavier Bertrand (LR) was re-elected as the President of the Hauts-de-France region. The latter confirmed that he intended to be a candidate for the French presidential elections in 2022. The results of the elections were a disappointment (*une déception*) for both Emmanuel Macron's party (LREM) and for Marine le Pen's party (RN).

The list of declared and possible candidates for the 2022 French presidential elections include (as at mid-January 2022):
Emmanuel Macron (LREM)
Marine Le Pen (RN)
Valérie Pécresse (LR)
Éric Zemmour (Right wing journalist and writer)
Anne Hidalgo (PS)
Jean-Luc Mélenchon (FI)
Yannick Jadot (MEP and ecologist)

PART 7

Some anecdotes, jokes, puns and quotations

Allez les Bleus!

Je reviens du stade de Twickenham

Encore quelques anecdotes, blagues, calembours et citations

Here are a final couple of anecdotes, followed by some tasteless but amusing French jokes and puns.

International Banking Conference

I once helped to organise a conference in Eastern Europe at which one of the expert speakers was a Frenchman. The proceedings were in English but there was simultaneous translation from English into the relevant East European language. The speaker had given the interpreters a written copy of his presentation and, although he did not read it verbatim, he kept to his outline script and there were no linguistic problems for the interpreters or for the audience. Our French expert spoke for a total of over two hours, including a question and answer session, with a break for coffee half-way through. He did an excellent job. He was truly an expert in his field. His English was excellent. As the only native English speaker, however, I could not help but pick up on the point that he was pronouncing "banking" as "bonking". "Today, I have the pleasure of talking to you about the two European Bonking Directives. France has many experienced international bonkers." And so, he went on bonking and bonking. Everyone else was oblivious to this special pronunciation. The audience was listening to the interpretation into their own language. The interpreters had their written text. In a moment of personal boredom with the intricacies of specific articles of the bonking rules, I made the mistake of explaining to a German expert who was to speak later in the day, the difference between banking and bonking. He now trained his ear more attentively to the talk on bonking and had difficulty in suppressing his amusement.
At the coffee break, I made a further error. I congratulated our French speaker on his excellent intervention thus far, but could he try to say banking rather than bonking, and he was amused by

my explanation. In giving the second part of his talk, he stumbled over every mention of the word bonking and tried his best to say banking, looking for reassurance each time from the panel of experts and notably from me and our German colleague. Later over lunch, when all was done and dusted, our French expert came up to me and said, *"If I have the choice in my life, I think I would prefer to be remembered, **not** as an expert in banking, **but** as an expert in bonking*!"

International Mixed Doubles

This truly was a mixture. My tennis partner was a French-speaking Belgian girl, and we were playing a match against two German male veterans. We played during the lunch break, so it was a one set match only. The German pair had rarely lost a match. We soon found out the reason. They both had semi-professional serves, and one of them thundered down his first serve like he was Boris Becker, serving as hard to my female partner as he did to me. She dreaded receiving serve when it was his service. Otherwise, the game was played in a reasonably amicable spirit, and we gave them a close match, but lost. My partner commented to me at the end of the match on how hard "Boris Becker's" serve had been. She translated directly from the French: *"Je ressentais le poids de ses balles (de tennis)."*
"I felt the weight of his balls!"

The Egyptian Mummy

A French archaeologist goes to Egypt and discovers a mummy. He decides to bring it back to Paris to undertake extensive research. He lays the mummy on a table in his laboratory. One night, working late, he thinks he hears the mummy trying to talk. The mummy is over 2,000 years old.

He puts his ear to the mummy's head and the mummy asks, "Is Johnny Hallyday still singing?"

(Unfortunately, not. Johnny Hallyday died in 2017. He burst on the scene in the 1960s as the French "Elvis" and was well-loved in France, continuing to appear on stage right up to the year of his death).

World Archery Contest

A contest has been organised to determine who is the best archer in the world. There are three finalists. The target is a human target with an apple on his head, standing 50 metres away.
The first contestant steps up to the mark. He composes himself, draws his bow, takes aim and releases his arrow. It plunges into the apple. The crowd roar with approval. He turns to the crowd and declares: "Je suis Guillaume Tell!"

A new apple is placed on top of the head of the human target. The next contestant steps up to the mark. He composes himself, draws his bow, takes aim and releases his arrow. It plunges into the apple. The crowd roar with approval. He turns to the crowd and declares: "Je suis Robin des Bois!"

A new apple is placed on top of the head of the human target.

The next contestant steps up to the mark. The crowd gasp. He is only three feet tall. He is unsteady on his feet. He lifts the huge bow, takes aim and releases his arrow. It pierces the heart of the human target. The crowd gasp. The little man turns to the crowd and declares: "Je suis Very Sorry!"

(I heard this joke on a French radio station):

Comment choisir les prénoms?

— Papa, pourquoi as-tu nommé mon frère Léon?
— Parce que ta maman aime Noël, et Léon, c'est une anagramme de Noël.
— Merci papa.
— De rien, Luc.

Les calembours/les jeux de mots

Two examples of puns cited by Henriette Walter in her book "*Le français dans tous les sens*".

(Une coquette d'âge mûr, miaudant devant un jeune homme):
— *Méfiez-vous, jeune homme, je suis rusée.*
— *Oh! Madame, c'est un < r > que vous vous donnez.*
(STENDHAL, *Correspondance*)

(Elle) Il me faut, disons le mot, cinquante mille francs…
(Lui) Par mois?
(Elle) Par vous ou par un autre!

(Sacha GUITRY)

Some French quotations

Jeanne d'Arc: *"Je suis la première pucelle de France; et les Anglais ne veulent que me faire brûler sur le bûcher."*

René Descartes: *"Je pense; donc je suis."* (That old chicken and egg conundrum).

Jean-Jacques Rousseau: *"L'homme est né libre..."* (Born Free – much later a hit for Matt Munro; and title of a hugely successful film about lions in Africa starring Bill Travers and Virginia Mackenna).

Louis XIV: *"L'Etat, c'est moi."* (I am the Sun God).

Louis XV: *"Après moi le déluge."* (I've made a mess of things).

Voltaire: *"Mais il faut cultiver notre jardin."* (We still need to work on our garden).

Louis XVI: *"Ma tête va tomber."* (Heads will roll; mine included).

Marie Antoinette: *"Qu'ils mangent de la brioche!"* (Let them eat cake).

Napoléon Bonaparte: *"J'ai mal à la tête."* (Not tonight, Joséphine).

Marcel Proust: *"J'avais mangé trop de madeleines dans mon enfance."* (I shouldn't have eaten so many cakes when I was younger).

Antoine de St. Exupéry: *"On ne voit bien qu'avec le coeur."* (from *Le Petit Prince*).

Jean-Paul Sartre: *"L'Enfer, c'est les autres."* (Hell is other people).

Roger Vadim: *"Et Dieu créa la femme."* (*Elle s'appelle Brigitte Bardot*).

Edith Piaf: *"Non, je ne regrette rien."* (If I had the chance, I'd do it all again).

Charles de Gaulle: *"Plus de 300 fromages. Je n'exagères pas."*

Jacques Brel: *"Ne me quitte pas..."* (If you go away...)

Sacha Distel: *"Yes, zose rrain dwops keep fallin on my ead. I must get myself un parapluie."*

Jane Birkin / Serge Gainsbourg: *"Je t'aime, moi non plus."* (Heavy breathing set to music).

Jacques Prévert: *"Le corps? Il court encore"* (from *"En Famille"* in *Spectacle*).

Marcel Pagnol: *"Telle est la vie des hommes. Quelques joies très vite effacées. Quelques inoubliables chagrins. Il n'est pas nécessaire de le dire aux enfants"* (from *Le Château de ma Mère*).

Michel Sardou: "*Le bon temps c'est quand? Quand on est vivant seulement.*"

Serge Gainsbourg (a little worse for drink during a French TV programme was asked what he thought of upcoming star Whitney Houston who was sitting near him): "*Je voudrais la baiser.*"
Interviewer (apologetically): "*He would like to kiss you.*"
Serge Gainsbourg insists: "*Non, non, je voudrais la baiser.*"

Eric Cantona: "*When the seagulls follow the trawler, it is because they think the sardines will be thrown into the sea.*"
Emmanuel Macron: "*Pour répondre aux variants (de la Covid-19), on voit que d'autres vaccins sont plus efficaces (que le vaccin AstraZenica)*" (le 9 mai 2021).
Eric Cantona (on being inducted into the Premier League's Hall of Fame): "*I am very happy and very proud, but at the same time I am not surprised*" (18 May 2021).

Appartement de Serge Gainsbourg
Rue de Verneuil 75006 Paris

PART 8

In Memory of George Voice

Aldershot 1915

In Memory of George Voice

If you should ever be in the town centre of Horsham, West Sussex, known as The Carfax, you will see the First World War Memorial, commemorating those Horsham residents who were killed in that Great War. Among the list of names in alphabetical order is inscribed that of G. Voice.

This is George Voice. He was the eldest son of Owen and Ada Mary Voice of 1 Linden Terrace. He was my father's oldest brother. Before enlisting in the Royal Sussex Regiment on the 9th November 1914, he worked for the Horsham Fire Brigade and lived in Horsham.

He was Sergeant George Voice G/7304 of 6th Battalion Royal West Kent Regiment 12th Division 37th Brigade. He died in France on 4th December 1917 at the age of 22.

He was mortally wounded by gunshot wounds to his shoulder and chest. He was taken prisoner on 30th November 1917, dying four days later at the German Grand Font Field Hospital. He had served in France since October 1916.

The Germans buried him first in their own plot in Esnes Cemetery. In 1921 his body was disinterred by the War Graves Commission and reburied in the British Cemetery in Honnechy, Northern France: PLOT 1 ROW A GRAVE 23

"(…) there's some corner of a foreign field
That is forever England" – *Rupert Brook*

"At the going down of the sun and in the morning,
We will remember them" – *Laurence Binyon*

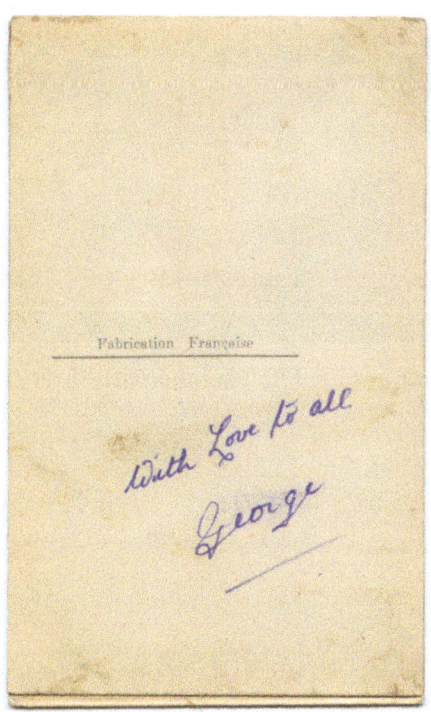

Queen's Own Royal Kent West Regiment

153

In Memory of
Sergeant GEORGE VOICE
Service Number: G7304
6th Bn. Queen's Own (Royal West Kent Regiment) who died
on 4th December 1917
Honnechy British Cemetery
I.A. 23

*The Cemetery is maintained by The Commonwealth War
Graves Commission*

HONNECHY BRITISH CEMETERY

There are over 450 casualties of the First World War (1914 to 1918) commemorated in this site.

Honnechy est un petit village français situé dans le département du Nord (59) et la région des Hauts-de-France (anciennement région Nord-Pas-de-Calais). Ses habitants sont appelés les Hunyclésiens et les Hunyclésiennes. The Municipality of Honnechy is located in the Hauts-de-France region. It has 556 residents known as "*Hunyclésiens*" and "*Hunyclésiennes*".

The Mayor of Honnechy is Mr. Bertrand Lefebvre who was elected in 2020 for a term of six years.

George Voice repose en paix avec ses compatriotes et parmi les Hunyclésiens.

The War Memorial, Carfax, Horsham, West Sussex

APPENDICES

Appendix 1
Visit to Normandy D-Day Landing Beaches

The **Normandy Landing Beaches** are located between Cherbourg in the West and Le Havre in the East: code-named **Utah, Omaha** (the American beaches**), Gold, Juno** and **Sword** (the British and Canadian beaches). We visited the following sites over a period of two to three days:

We stayed in a hotel at Ouistreham for two nights and visited both the **Merville German Gun Battery Site** and **Pegasus Bridge**. We then based ourselves at a hotel in **Bayeux** for two or three more nights. Home of the Bayeux Tapestry (famous 11th century embroidery of the events leading up to and including the Conquest of Britain by William the Conqueror); and the Norman Cathedral. There are several War museums, but we did not visit these on this trip.

We visited the **British and Commonwealth World War II Cemetery in Bayeux**. Over 4,500 graves. Opposite is the Bayeux Memorial to the Missing with no known graves. The Latin inscription above translates as "William conquered us; we helped to liberate your country."

There is an impressive statue of **General Eisenhower**, the allied supreme commander of the D-Day invasion, on a roundabout on the outskirts of town.

Arromanches: the remains of the **Mulberry harbour** can be seen at low-tide. The **D-Day Museum** has a model of the harbour and detailed explanations are given as to its construction and how it was floated over from Britain. The **360 degree cinema** on the cliff top overlooking the harbour and town gives an impressive and emotional show of images and sounds, immersing you in the action. You can park here and walk down to the harbour and museum.

The **German Gun Battery at Longues-sur-Mer**: the impressive remains of four huge German guns; and the lookout bunker on the cliff edge. Beware of midges/biting insects around the bunker.

The **American Cemetery at Saint-Laurent-sur-Mer** which

overlooks part of **Omaha beach**. It is possible to walk down from the cemetery to the beach.

Pointe du Hoc: where US rangers scaled the cliff on D-Day. The site is full of bomb craters like the surface of the moon. The German artillery guns were directed at Utah and Omaha beach and had to be eliminated prior to the US landings there.

Sainte-Mère-Église: US paratroopers parachuted behind Utah beach, but some came down around this village. John Steele landed on the church steeple, commemorated still by a dummy parachutist hanging from the steeple. There is an **American Airborne glider museum** close by. Lots of souvenir shops here selling World War Two memorabilia.

Utah Beach: **Utah beach museum** housed in the German bunker; and you can see examples of Rommel's "asparagus" – barbed wire obstacles to thwart a landing. Brigadier Theodore Roosevelt jr. led the USA troops ashore here on D-Day. He died 12 days later of a heart attack and is buried in the American Cemetery.

The **German Cemetery** at **la Cambe**. Contrast the dark sombre aspect and layout of this cemetery with that of the vast expanse of white gravestones at the American cemetery.

Two films: The Longest Day 1962
Saving Private Ryan 1998

There are many books on D-Day. The Pitkin series of guides are an excellent introduction.
D-Day and the Battle of Normandy 1944 Pitkin
ISBN 085372-682-5

PS: The newly completed British Normandy Memorial, overlooking Gold Beach at Ver-sur-mer, was officially opened on 6 June 2021, the 77th anniversary of the D-Day landings.

Map of Normandy D-Day Landing Beaches (see opposite)

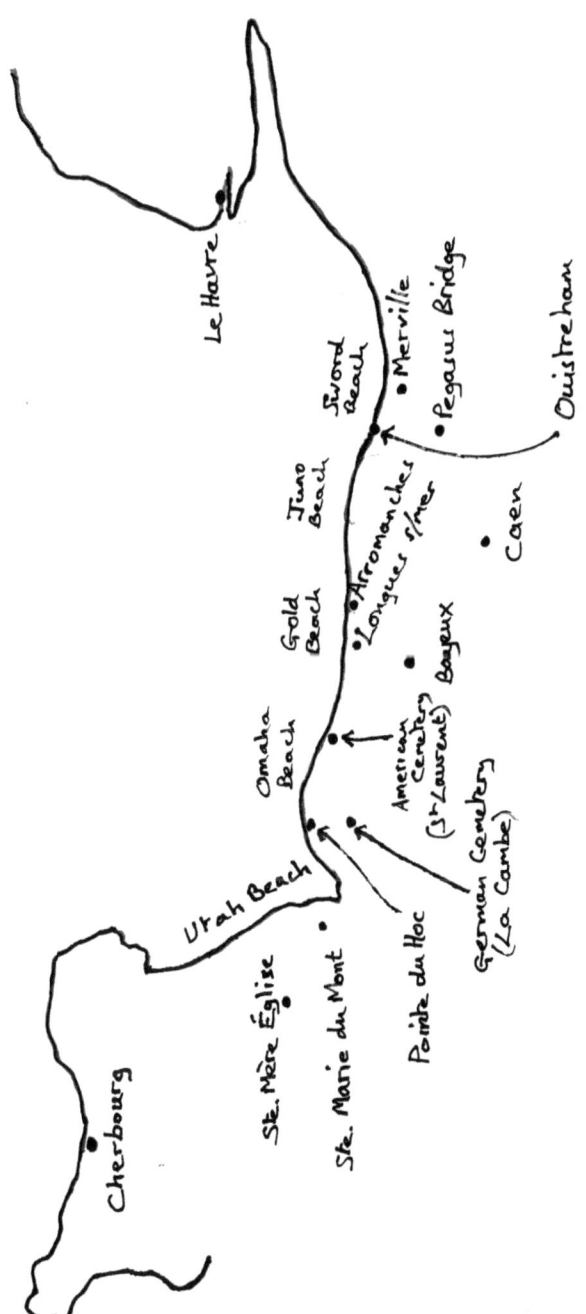

Le Havre

Sword Beach

Merville

Pegasus Bridge

Ouistreham

Juno Beach

Longues s/mer

Arromanches

Caen

Gold Beach

Omaha Beach

American Cemetery (St-Laurent)

Bayeux

German Cemetery (La Cambe)

Utah Beach

Pointe du Hoc

Ste. Marie du Mont

Ste. Mère Église

Cherbourg

Appendix 2
Apple Tarte Tatin Recipe

For the pastry: ready-made puff pastry
For the filling:
Six Cox or four Granny Smith apples, peeled, cored and cut into 8-12 wedges.
¼ lemon
110g/4oz caster sugar
110g/4oz butter

Method
*Preheat the oven to 250C/500F/Gas 9
*For the filling, place the apple wedges in a bowl, squeeze the lemon juice over them and toss them gently
*Sprinkle 85g/3oz of the sugar in a heavy-bottomed pan and place on the hob over a medium heat, turning the pan frequently and making sure the sugar doesn't burn. Allow the sugar to caramelise a little and become a pale golden brown, then remove from the heat and arrange the drained apple pieces in one layer over the bottom of the pan.
*Place the pan in the oven and bake until the apples have softened a bit and started to release some liquid –about 10 minutes.
*Remove from the oven and sprinkle over the remaining sugar and dot the butter on top. Roll out the pastry to fit the pan and return to the oven, turn the heat down to 220C/425F/Gas 7 and bake until the pastry is golden brown – about 20 minutes. Remove from the oven and leave to rest for a minute or two.
* Take a heatproof serving dish that is generously larger than the pan on all sides and place over the pan. Protecting your hands with a dry folded tea-towel, and holding the dish and pan firmly together, quickly and carefully flip the pan and the dish so that the pan is on top. Tap the pan sharply a few times all round with a wooden spoon, then lift off. The tart should be left on the serving dish with the apple on top.

*Cut into appropriate portions. Eat as is, or serve with vanilla ice-cream or whipped cream.

Recipe provided, and kindly permitted to be reproduced here, by **Head Chef, Barry Scarborough**, at Ghyll Manor Hotel & Restaurant, Rusper nr. Horsham, West Sussex.

Appendix 3
French words for 31 body parts:

La cheville	ankle	Le nez	nose
La jambe	leg	Une oreille	ear
La narine	nostril	La tête	head
Un oeil	eye	Un cil	eyelash
Le mollet	calf	La joue	cheek
La cuisse	thigh	La lèvre	lip
La bouche	mouth	La langue	tongue
Le coude	elbow	Le menton	chin
Le front	forehead	La peau	skin
La main	hand	Le doigt	finger
Un ongle	nail	Une épaule	shoulder
Le ventre	stomach	Un os	bone
Le sein	breast	Le bras	arm
La dent	tooth	Le genou	knee
Le dos	back	Le cou	neck
Le nombril	belly button/ navel		

Solution to word search on page 42: CALVADOS (French *département* N⁰14; and *du calvados* is apple brandy):

7/3	C
8/4	A
9/12	L
8/6	V
4/10	A
4/11	D
2/11	O
9/9	S

OTHER BODY PARTS

Le sourcil	eyebrow	L'orteil	toe
Le foie	liver	Les reins	kidneys
Le pouce	thumb	Les poumons	lungs
Le coeur	heart	Le derrière Les fesses	behind buttocks
Le poing	fist	Le poignet	wrist
L'épine	spine	Le pancréas	pancreas

Les paupières	eyelids
Les gencives	gums
La poitrine	chest
Le cerveau	brain
La mâchoire	jaw
Le talon	heel

Appendix 4
Quel temps fait-il?

The French think the British are obsessed with the weather. There is no sun in the UK. It rains a lot.

La météo, la prévision du temps – weather forecast.

Ils avaient prévu de la pluie ce matin. They forecast rain this morning.

Heureusement ils se sont plantés! Fortunately, they got it wrong!

Un parapluie: an umbrella.

Il pleut un peu beaucoup chez nous: It rains a bit too much at home.

Le soleil nous manque: There's not enough sun / we miss the sunshine.

Après la pluie, le beau temps: Every cloud has a silver lining.

Le soleil brille sur les fidèles: The sun shines on the righteous.

Qu'est-ce qu'il fait beau aujourd'hui!: What a beautiful day!

Du soleil!: sunshine!

Quel beau jour ensoleillé!: What a fine sunny day!

Vous êtes le soleil de ma vie: You are the sunshine of my life;

Une éclaircie: a clear patch in the sky;

Un arc-en-ciel: a rainbow.

Il fait un beau temps: The weather is fine;

Il fait chaud: It's hot;

Une canicule: a heatwave;

Mettez-vous à l'ombre: Go in the shade [*l'ombre* can also mean *shadow*].

Il fait un mauvais temps: The weather is bad;

Il fait un froid de canard: It's very cold;

Ça caille!: It's freezing!

Elle est frileuse/il est frileux: She / he is sensitive to the cold weather.

La température baisse: The temperature is falling. *Il fait moins de 12° degrés*: it's less than 12° degrees (Celsius);

Il fait plus frais: it is cooler;

Il va pleuvoir: It's going to rain;

Le ciel est couvert: the sky is overcast;

C'est nuageux: it's cloudy;

Des nuages: clouds.

Il pleut sans cesse, il pleut à verse, il pleut des cordes, des hallebardes (it's raining hard/pouring down);

Une averse: a sudden shower;

Une ondée: heavy shower;

Une giboulée: a downpour followed by sunshine; *Il fait un après-midi de chien:* it's a miserable afternoon;

Il fait un temps comme en Angleterre: just like the weather in England;

De la pluie diluvienne: torrential rain;

Un pays pluvieux: a rainy country;

Une journée pluvieuse: a rainy day;

Il grêle: it is hailing;

La grêle: hail;

Des grêlons: hail-stones;

Il fait du brouillard: It's foggy;

La brume: mist;

Le vent se lève: The wind is getting up;

Il fait un vent fort: it's very windy;

Un tourbillion/une trombe: whirlwind;

Un typhon: typhoon;

Un ouragan: hurricane;

Des coups de foudre/des éclairs: lightning;

Des coups de tonnerre: thunder;

Un orage/une tempête: a storm [*le coup de foudre* can also mean *love at first sight*];

Il neige: It's snowing;

Des boules de neige: snow balls;

Du verglas: ice on the roads;

Vigilance inondations et <u>crues</u>: warning of floods and <u>rising river levels</u>;

La Seine est en crue: the water level of the River Seine is rising;

Une mousson: monsoon;

Un tremblement de terre/un séisme: earthquake; *Un tsunami:*

Les intempéries: bad weather;

Un temps ou un climat inclément: harsh weather or climate.

Appendix 5
Some Animal Expressions

Un chat = a cat
Il n'y a pas un chat: The place is deserted.
J'ai un chat dans la gorge: I've got a frog in my throat.
Il appelle un chat un chat: He calls a spade a spade.
Je donne ma langue au chat: I give in guessing; what is it?
Il n'y a pas de quoi fouetter un chat: It's nothing to write home about.
J'ai d'autres chats à fouetter: I've other fish to fry.

Un chien = a dog
Elles s'entendent comme chien et chat: they are always arguing.
Ils vivent comme chien et chat: They are completely in the dark (i.e., not informed).
Il fait un temps de chien: The weather is miserable.
Elle a du chien: She is hot (stuff).
Il mène une vie de chien: His life is miserable and difficult.
J'ai un faim de loup (wolf): I am ravenously hungry.
Ils sont amis comme cochons (pigs): They are close friends/They get on like a house on fire.
Poser un lapin (rabbit) à qqn: to stand someone up/to not turn up for a date;
Se faire poser un lapin: to be stood up;
Plaquer qqn. and larguer qqn.: both mean to dump someone (*l'espion qui m'a larguée: The spy who dumped me*).
Être myope comme une taupe (lit. short-sighted as a mole): to be as blind as a bat;
Rusé(e) comme un renard: sly as a fox;
Malin (maligne) comme un singe: a clever monkey;
Fainéant(e) comme une couleuvre: as lazy as a grass snake.
Elle a dû avaler des couleuvres (lit. swallow grass snakes): She had to accept criticism or reproach without protesting/she had to bite her lip/take it on the chin.

*Ménager la chèvre et le chou (*lit. manage the goat and the cabbage): to manage diplomatically/keep happy two conflicting people or interests.

Être à cheval sur l'étiquette: To be a stickler for good manners;

Miser sur le mauvais cheval: To back the wrong horse;

La brebis galeuse de la famille: The black sheep of the family;

Un bouc émissaire: a scapegoat;

Un cobaye: a guinea pig (but the pet animal is *le cochon d'Inde*);

*Il y a anguille (*an eel*) sous roche*: I smell a rat/there's something fishy going on.

*Il fait des queues de poisson (*fish tails): He's driving from side to side/eratically/weaving in and out.

*Quelle mouche (*fly*) t'a piqué(e)?* Whose got up your nose?

Prendre la mouche: to fly off the handle;

*J'ai des fourmis (*ants*) dans la jambe:* I've got pins and needles;

*Revenons à nos moutons (*sheep): Let's get back to the subject;

*J'ai le cafard (*lit. cockroach*):* I'm feeling depressed / fed up.

*Je transpire comme un boeuf (*lit. a cow*):* I'm sweating like a pig;

Elle est bavarde comme une pie: She's as chatty as a magpie;

C'est un drôle de zèbre: He's a strange bloke;

Je ne veux pas mettre la charrue devant les boeufs: I don't want to put the cart before the horse (lit. the plough before the oxen);

Ne faites pas l'autruche (ostrich): Don't bury your head in the sand/Don't pretend it's not happening;

*Être le dindon (*turkey*) de la farce:* to be made to look a fool/to be the laughing stock;

Cessez d'être un mouton dans le troupeau! Stop doing what everyone else does/make your own decisions; *n'aboyez pas avec la meute:* don't bark with the pack.

(*La vénerie* is the science of hunting; *la chasse aux gibiers* hunting/game shooting *chasser* is to hunt; *la chasse à courre* is hunting with a pack of dogs; *la chasse à la glu* is hunting using bird lime/now forbidden in Europe; *un piège* is a trap and *tendre un piège* is to set a trap; *la chasse aux renards* (fox hunting – now illegal in UK); *le gavage/le forcing* is the force feeding of geese to enlarge their livers (*foie*) for the production of *pâté de foie gras*; *braconner* is to poach; *un braconnier* is a poacher and *le braconnage* is poaching).

Appendix 6
Arms and Legs and other body parts

Many French expressions are formed using body parts. Here is a selection:

Avoir le bras long: to have influence/to be well connected;

Mon bras droit: my trusted assistant;

Un bras de fer: arm wrestling contest/trial of strength/power struggle;

Aux bras ouverts: with open arms;

Le bras d'honneur: the French equivalent of our V sign;

L'équipe de France n'a pas baissé les bras: The French team did not give up;

Cela me fait une belle jambe: That's a fat lot of good to me;

Elle m'a tenu la jambe pendant si longtemps que j'ai failli manquer le train: She kept me talking so long I nearly missed my train;

Je vais me dégourdir les jambes: I'm going to stretch my legs;

Elle s'est cassé la jambe: she broke her leg;

Il a une entorse à la cheville: he has sprained his ankle;

Vous donnez des entorses à la réalité/à la vérité: you are twisting the facts;

Elle a les jambes en X: she is knock-kneed;

Le bossu de Notre-Dame: the hunchback of Notre-Dame;

Il s'est mis les pieds dans le plat: He has put his foot in it;

Tu me casses les pieds/la tête: You are annoying/boring me/getting on my nerves;

Je joue comme un pied: I am playing very badly;

Il a un pied dans la fosse: He's got one foot in the grave;

Cela te saute aux yeux: It's staring you in the face;

Elle est partie du pied gauche: She has started off on the wrong foot;

Je me suis levé(e) du pied gauche: I got out of bed on the wrong side;

Ils traînent les pieds: They are lagging behind, taking their time, dragging their feet.

Ils piétinent: They are not making any progress.

Europe 1 a mis à pied un de ses journalistes: Europe 1 has suspended the activity of one of its reporters.

Cela m'a coûté les yeux de la tête: That has cost me an arm and a leg;

Il a des petits yeux/il a mal aux cheveux/il a une gueule de bois: He has a hangover;

Il a froid aux yeux: He is scared;

J'ai des valises sous les yeux: I've got bags under my eyes;

Cela me fait froid dans le dos: That sends a shiver down my spine;

Casser du sucre sur le dos de qqn.: to talk about someone behind their back;

Mettre le nez dans les affaires des autres: to stick one's nose in other people's business;

Arrête de creuser dans le nez: Stop picking your nose!

Ne ronge pas tes ongles: Don't bite your nails;

Faire une tête: to pull a long face; to look glum;

Faire la (mauvaise) tête: to sulk;

Ils nous marchent sur la tête: They are walking all over us.

Des taches de rousseurs (freckles); *des fossettes* (dimples); *un grain de beauté* (beauty spot or mole); *des boutons* (spots); *des ampoules* (are blisters as well as light bulbs; *des bleus/des contusions* (bruises).

Tu te payes de ma tête: You are making a fool of me/making fun of me;

J'ai une dent contre lui: I have a bone to pick with him/I bear him a grudge;

Il est endetté jusqu'au cou: He's up to his eyeballs in debt;

Manger sur le pouce: to have a snack/a quick bite to eat; to eat on the go;

Donner le coup de pouce à qqch.: to put the finishing touches to something;

Donner un coup de main à qqn.: to give someone a helping hand;

Vous êtes entre de bonnes mains: You are in good hands;

Déposer une main courante: to report an incident to the police;

(*Une main courante* is an incident log-book; a hand rail).

Le talon d'Achilles: Achilles heel;

Les Bleus ont renoncé à <u>mettre un genou à terre</u> (the French football team decided not "<u>to take the knee</u>") *avant le coup d'envoi du match contre l'Allemagne.*

Appendix 7
Some Idiomatic Phrases and Vocabulary

Qu'ils arrêtent de <u>casser du sucre sur</u> la ville de Trappe: They should stop running down/casting aspersions on the town of Trappe.
Être soupe au lait: to have a short fuse; *il est soupe au lait*.
Pétér un plomb: to blow a fuse/lose one's temper;
Vouloir le beurre et le prix du beurre: to want one's cake and eat it;
Bricoler / faire du bricolage: to potter about/do DIY;
C'est la cerise sur le gâteau: It's the icing on the cake;
La chasse aux sorcières: a witch hunt;
Tirer son épingle du jeu: to extricate oneself from a difficult situation without loss;
Être tiré(e) à quatre épingles, être endimanché(e), être sur son trente et un: to be dressed to the nines, done up like a dog's dinner, in one's Sunday best (clothes);
Rentrer bredouille: to come home empty-handed; *ils sont rentrés bredouille(<u>s</u>)*;
La soirée bat son plein: The evening (do) is in full swing;
Mon coeur bat la chamade: My heart is going like the clappers;
Faire la grasse matinée: to have a lie-in;
Cela me brise le coeur; je suis navré(e): It breaks my heart; I'm heartbroken;
Battre le fer pendant qu'il est chaud: to strike while the iron is hot/make hay while the sun shines;
J'ai la trouille, j'ai la frousse, j'ai le trac (butterflies in my stomach) = *j'ai peur/tu me fais peur*: I am scared/you scare me;
Avoir un cadavre (a corpse) dans le placard: to have a skeleton in the cupboard;
Un chauffard qui prend la fuite: a hit and run driver;
Faire une queue de poisson: to cut in sharply in front of another car;
Avancer en accordéon: to advance concertina fashion in traffic;
Se faufiler en voiture dans les rues: to weave in and out of the streets;
Brûler un feu rouge/griller les feux: to go through a red traffic light; to jump the lights;

Etre coincé(e) dans un embouteillage/dans un bouchon: to be stuck in a traffic jam;

Quel est le numéro d'immatriculation de votre voiture? What's your car reg?

Un alcotest: a breathalyser;

Mettre en fourrière un animal abandonné; une voiture illégalement garée: to impound a stray animal; an illegally parked car;

Il ne fait pas le poids: He's not up to the job;

Son prognostic vital n'est pas engagé: His/Her condition is not life-threatening;

On tourne en rond! We are going round in circles (we are getting nowhere)!

Elle brille par son absence: Her absence is conspicuous;

Votre braguette est déboutonnée!: Your flies are undone;

Tu m'agaces, tu m'énerves, tu m'embêtes: You are annoying me, getting on my nerves;

Verbaliser qqn.: to give someone an on-the-spot fine; similarly, *dresser une contravention* or *un procès-verbal à qqn.* (usually for a minor parking, driving offence; for not wearing a mask etc.);

Il s'est fait virer de son job: He got fired from his job (*virer qqn., renvoyer qqn., congédier qqn., limoger qqn.* to sack/fire/dismiss someone);

licencier qqn.: to make someone redundant;

Monter au créneau: to accept one's responsibility; put one's head above the parapet; to step up to the plate; *un créneau* is an opening, a niche in the market, an opportunity;

Pendre la crémaillère: to have a house-warming meal or party;

Rouler qqn. (dans la farine): to con, swindle someone; *se faire rouler* to be conned; *ils se sont fait rouler:* they were conned;

C'est de l'arnaque/c'est du vol: It's daylight robbery;

Une arnaque: a scam, con, rip-off;

Un escroc, un arnaqueur: a scammer, crook, swindler;

Arnaquer, escroquer: to scam, con, swindle;

C'est la pagaille: It's chaos.

Appendix 8
Some Computer/TV/Phone Vocabulary

L'informatique (computer science, computer industry, data processing and transmission);
L'internet;
Être sur les réseaux/médias sociaux;
Être sur Twitter, Facebook, Instagram, YouTube, Twitch;
Tweeter qqn./twitter qqn.; un tweet/un twitt; les tweets/les twitts; un tweeteur/une tweeteuse (c'est qqn. qui tweete ou twitte);
Les youtubeurs;
Une chaîne YouTube: YouTube channel;
Une chaîne de télévision: TV channel;
Un influenceur/une influenceuse;
500.000 dossiers médicaux ont fuité suite à une cyberattaque;
Les pirates d'internet: internet hackers;
Son site internet s'est fait pirater: has been hacked;
Télécharger une appli(cation): download an app;
Le gouvernement s'adresse aux jeunes sur Twitch;
Envoyer par mail, un mail (un courriel), un message SMS, un texto;
Du courrier indésirable, du pourriel, un message spam: spam/junk mail;
L'incroyable bug du 13h de TF1; bug = problème technique;
La star de la téléréalité Kim Kardashian;
Les deepfakes: in a video, a politician or famous person has his or her face imposed on that of another; and/or fake words are attributed. *Truquer* to fake; *un masque numérique* a digital mask.
Le cyberharcèlement: cyber bullying/harassment; *La haine en ligne:* hatred on line;
La désinformation: disinformation;
Un selfie;
La diffusion de photos intimes sur internet;
L'arobase: @
Les smileys ☺☺☺ *les binettes* ☺☺☺ *les frimousses;*
Les émoticônes;
Les émojis;

Les plateformes de streaming;

Les plateaux de télévision: TV panels/platforms;

Devrait-on laisser les appareils en veille (stand-by) *ou les éteindre?*
Should we leave our devices on stand-by or turn them off?

Imprimer un document: to print a document;

L'imprimante: printer;

La télécommande/le zappeur: the remote control;

Le logiciel: software;

Le matériel: hardware;

Une transmission en duplex: two-way live transmission;

Une transmission en clair: free-to-air broadcast;

Une transmission/émission en direct: live broadcast;

Une transmission/émission en différé: recorded broadcast;

Environ 90% des foyers français sont équipés de smartphones et environ 90 % des adolescents en possèdent un.

Un feuilleton: TV soap, TV series;

Flouter une photo ou un film – to alter/doctor a photo or film using software to eliminate or hide details (a name, facial blemishes etc);

Truquer une photo: to fake a photo;

Les jeux vidéo: video games.

Appendix 9
Some Faux Amis and other interesting words

Les frites are chips; *les chips* (pronounced *sheeps*) are crisps.
Un car is a touring coach and *un car scolaire* is a school bus. *L'autobus/ le bus* is the single decker bus in town. *La voiture* is of course a car, *la voiture-balai* (sweeps up the Tour de France riders who cannot continue); *un camping-car; le co-voiturage* is car-sharing.
La prescription statute of limitations/prescription; someone who has committed a crime over thirty years ago may try to *invoquer la prescription* (invoke the statute of limitations); *un médecin prescrit un programme de traitement (*a doctor prescribes a course of treatment); *une prescription médicale* contains medical instructions.
Une ordonnance is a doctor's prescription you take to *la pharmacie* in order to get your prescribed *médicaments (*medecines).
Un préservatif is a condom; *les conservateurs* are jam preservatives.
L'entretien can mean both *la conversation* and *la conservation* (maintenance/also *le maintien*).
Le préjudice d'un cambriolage is the <u>amount stolen</u> in a break-in; *préjugé(e), partial(e)* and *le parti pris* is prejudiced, biased.
En fait, in fact, actually; *en effet*, indeed, in effect; *tout à fait*, indeed, exactly; *au fait*, after all.
Actuellement is currently; *à l'heure actuelle:* at the current time; *actualiser un rapport*: to bring a report up to date; *les actualités/ les informations* is The (TV) News; *mettre à jour mon courrier* is to update my correspondence; *tenir qqn. au courant* is to keep someone informed; *être au courant* is to know about something; to be up to date on an issue; *faire le point (de/sur):* to take stock (of).
Aveugle: blind; *la cécité:* blindness; *sourd(e)*: deaf; *la surdité:* deafness.
Du tissu: cloth *(du tissu de laine:* woollen cloth*)*; *des mouchoirs en papier/des Kleenex:* tissues; *un tissu de mensonges*: a tissue/pack of lies.
La formation = training.
La confection is clothes-making; *les confiseries* are confectionery and *les bonbons* are sweets/candies.
Le conditionnement is packaging (of a product*)*.

Emballer un cadeau: to wrap up a present.

Décevoir is to disappoint. *Je suis déçu(e)*: I am disappointed; *la déception* is disappointment; *tromper* is to deceive; *je me suis trompé(e)*: I was mistaken; *il a trompé sa femme:* he was unfaithful to his wife/ deceived his wife.

Du carton is cardboard; *un carton* is a cardboard box but in football the referee shows *(l'arbitre montre) un carton jaune (*yellow card) and *un carton rouge (*red card*)*.

Une chambre is a bedroom in a hotel and house *(chambre à coucher); une pièce* is a room in a house for example *cette maison a six pièces (y compris la salle de bain et la cuisine); une pièce de monnaie* (coin*); une pièce de théâtre (*play*); une pièce détachée (*spare part*); la pièce de résistance; une pièce d'identité* (ID card or passport). A piece can be *un morceau (de gâteau); une tranche* (slice) *de pain/un bout de pain; nous avons toujours un bon bout de chemin à faire* (we still have a good way to go); *les parties d'une machine* (the parts of a machine).

Une boîte can refer to the factory, office, shop, place where you work*; une boîte de nuit* is a night club; *une boîte* can be a box or a tin; *une cannette de Coca Cola, de Fanta, d'Orangina; une boîte d'allumettes* is a box of matches; *une boîte à malices* is a box of surprises and *une boîte de petits pois* is a tin of peas.

Une prune is a plum; *un pruneau* is a prune.

Le box is a lock-up garage, a horse-box and a cubicle; *le box de vaccination; le box des accusés* is the dock (stand for the accused) in a court; *la boxe* is boxing and *le catch* is wrestling.

Une cascade is a waterfall but *un cascadeur* is a stunt man.

L'isolement means loneliness or isolation; *s'isoler* is to isolate: *si vous êtes testé positif au coronavirus, vous devez vous isoler pendant dix jours; je me sens isolé(e)* is I feel lonely.

L'isolation means insulation.

Le traître is a traitor; *le traiteur* is a food caterer.

Ce n'est pas évident: It's not obvious/it's not <u>easy</u>.

La pêche is a peach; *un pêcher* is a peach tree but *la pêche* is also fishing. *Pêcher/aller à la pêche* is to go fishing; *un pêcheur/une pêcheuse*: fisherman/woman.

Pécher is to sin; *un pécheur* is a sinner/*une pécheresse* a female sinner.

Une grappe de raisins is a bunch of grapes; *un régime de bananes* is a bunch of bananas; *suivre un régime* is to go on a diet.

Des élections anticipées are elections held earlier than planned; the verbs *prévoir* (to foresee), *envisager*, and *s'attendre à (*to expect*)* can all mean to anticipate.

Les conséquences éventuelles are possible consequences.

Éventuellement means possibly; *tôt ou tard* means eventually, sooner or later.

Prématuré (e) means premature ; *controversé (e)* means controversial.

Les prix chocs: low prices; *éviter un choc frontal:* avoid a head-on collision; *le choc entre PSG et Marseille est reporté* (the clash between PSG and Marseille has been postponed).

Une situation inédite: unprecedented/extraordinary situation.

*Etre sidéré(e), abasourdi(e), estomaqué(e) (*flabbergasted, dumbstruck*) choqué(e), étonné(e).*

Je suis stupéfait(e): amazed, stunned;

Je suis stupéfié(e) par qqch; cela m'a stupéfié(e);

C'est hallucinant/c'est ahurissant: incredible, staggering, mind-blowing, mind-boggling;

C'est époustoufflant: astonishing;

Un contrôle inopiné is an unexpected, sudden, without prior warning inspection*;*

Sensible is sensitive; *raisonnable* is sensible;

Il est sorti indemne de l'accident: uninjured, undamaged, without loss;

Le saut à l'élastique: bungee jumping;

Le parkours: urban jumping;

Le deltaplane: hang-gliding;

Les enfants sont énergiques: the children are energetic;

Les fournisseurs énergétiques: energy suppliers;

Un événement incontournable: an unmissable event;

À ne pas contourner: not to be missed, *à ne pas manquer;*

Contourner un obstacle: to avoid/go round an obstacle;

Etre sceptique: sceptical; *méfiant(e)/défiant(e):* mistrustful/distrustful;

Je me méfie de lui: I don't trust him/I'm wary of him; *méfiez-vous des pickpockets:* beware of pickpockets;

Un photographe: photographer; *une photo(graphie):* photograph;

Sympathique: kind, nice; *compatissant*: compassionate, sympathetic;
Versatile/lunatique: mercurial, unreliable, unstable;
Un agenda: diary; *l'ordre du jour*: the agenda;
Un store: blind, awning; *une boutique, un magasin*: store;
Aider: to help; assister (à): to be present at;
Cultiver is to grow, to cultivate. *Un homme cultivé* is an educated man. *La culture* is cultivation and culture (art, films, plays etc.). *Les cultures* are crops; *la culture physique* is physical/weight training.

Appendix 10
Argot (slang words) and Colloquial words

Every *milieu* has its own set of vocabulary but here are a few words in common, everyday use. Students and young people generally are likely to use slang words more frequently than older people. But most of the following words are in everyday use, and you need to be able to understand them, even if there is no need for you to use them. None of these words will shock.

Un bouquin, un livre: book;

Du fric, de l'argent: money/dough/dosh (also *du pognon, de l'oseille, des sous*);

Les flics, les agents de police (policiers, gendarmes, CRS): the cops;

Une bagnole, une voiture: car/banger;

La bécane, une bicyclette, le vélo: bike, bicycle;

Une piaule, une chambre: room/bed–sit/digs;

La bouffe/la boustifaille, de la nourriture: food/grub/nosh;

Bouffer = *manger* = to eat;

Prendre un pot, boire un coup (= to go for a drink);

Roupiller = *dormir* = to sleep;

Rouspéter = *se plaindre* = to complain;

Le toubib	le médecin	doctor
Mon frangin	mon frère	my brother
Ma frangine	ma soeur	my sister
Ma belle-doche	ma belle–mère	my mother–in–law

Les gosses, les gamins/gamines, les mômes all mean kids (*les enfants*);

Un mec, un type, un gonze, un zig/zigue are words for bloke, geezer;

Une gonzesse, une poule, une nana are words for a woman;

C'est nickel, c'est royal, c'est top, c'est génial It's great, brilliant;

Enfilez (= mettez) votre pull, sweater, gilet put on your jumper, pullover;

Bosser: to work/work hard; *potasser*: to swot for an exam; *sécher les cours*: to skip lessons; *faire l'école buissonnière*: to play truant;

Mon boulot, mon job, mon travail: my job/work;

Un piston is a friend in high places. *Faire du piston* or *se faire pistonner* is to make use of this friend to advance your career.

Se balader (faire une promenade à pied), se balader en voiture (faire une promenade en voiture) is to go for a walk, a drive.

Un chauffard is a reckless driver, a road hog.

Tu piges? Tu comprends? Do you get it?

Il est gonflé: he's got a nerve; he's made up; he's full of himself;

Il est culotté, il a du culot: He's got a nerve, he's got some cheek;

Mon pote, mon copain/ma copine: my mate, my friend;

Son mec/son Jules et sa Julie/sa Nana = her boyfriend and his girlfriend;

Je suis fauché(e)/à sec; je n'ai plus de sous; je n'ai plus un rond: I'm broke/short of money.

Faites gaffe! Watch it! Watch out!

Un dérapage = a slip up, error; *une bavure* = a cock-up;

Le videur d'une boîte de nuit: a night club bouncer; *vider qqn.:* to throw someone out;

J'en ai ras le bol = I am fed up = *j'en ai marre;*

Piquer, chiper and *choper* mean to pinch, to steal;

Il est dingue, c'est dingue: he is crazy/it is crazy;

Cinglé(e), cintré(e), timbré(e), fada, toqué(e): stupid, crazy;

Il est bourré, paf, rond: he is drunk (*ivre, soûl*);

La douloureuse (= l'addition), s'il vous plaît: the bill (lit. the painful bit), please;

Avoir du pot is to be lucky; *prendre un pot* is to go for a drink;

Avoir de la guigne, de la poisse is to have bad luck; *la scoumoune* is persistent bad luck;

Louper/rater le train, un examen: to miss the train, fail an exam [*manquer le train/échouer à un examen (échouer* also means to run aground of a ship: *l'échouement du navire au canal de Suez)*].

Etre ringard(e): to be cheesy, out of date;

Les fringues: clothes;

Un flingue: a gun, firearm;

Draguer les filles: to chat up/chase girls;

Un coureur de jupons: a womaniser;

Se planter: to fail, to mess up, to get wrong; *ils se sont plantés*: they failed; *je me suis planté en maths/à mon examen de maths* (I failed/messed up my maths exam); *tu t'es planté, c'est 50 euros pas 35 euros*: You've got it wrong, it's 50 not 30 euros.

Un ordinateur peut se planter: a computer can crash;

Il s'est planté en voiture: he crashed his car;

Elle s'est plantée devant la porte de l'immeuble: she's stood in front of the door of the building (she's standing there firmly without moving);

Un braqueur/une braqueuse: an armed robber;

<u>Un fourgon blindé</u> *a été braqué ce matin à Lyon par trois à quatre individus armés:* an <u>armoured/bullet proof/security vehicle</u> was attacked by three or four armed robbers this morning in Lyon.

Les braqueurs ont pris la fuite après avoir dérobé de l'argent, de l'or et des bijoux: The armed robbers fled having stolen money, gold and jewellery.

Un braquage: an armed robbery;

Un indic (indicateur), une balance, un mouchard, un corbeau are all words for an informer *(un délateur/une délatrice, un dénonciateur/une dénonciatrice); dénoncer qqn, balancer qqn:* to inform on someone);

Je suis paumé(e): I am lost;

Des couche-tôt et des couche-tard (people who go to bed early and late);

Je m'en fous/je m'en fiche/je m'en moque: I don't give a damn/I don't care.

Je suis crevé(e): I am knackered/very tired;

Je crève de faim: I could eat a horse;

Éreinté(e): dog-tired;

Épuisé(e): exhausted.

Appendix 11
Le Coronavirus/la Covid-19

Faites-vous vacciner!

Le Coronavirus/la Covid-19

Une épidémie/une pandémie/cette crise sanitaire mondiale
Les chiffres, les statistiques, les courbes, les graphiques, les tableaux
exposés, interpretés et expliqués par les scientifiques, le ministre de la Santé (Olivier Véran), le Premier ministre (Jean Castex), le Président de la République (Emmanuel Macron), le Conseil de Défense, le directeur général de la santé, les infectiologues, les épidémiologistes, les virologues, les médecins, les infirmiers, les journalistes de TV et de presse, les citoyens français ou républicains.

<u>Le tableau de bord (au 13 avril 2021)</u>
Nombre de nouveaux cas confirmés: 39.113
Nombre de personnes hospitalisées: 31.226
Nombre de patients en réanimation: 5.912
Décès (en 24h/total): 324/99.508
Nombre de vaccinations:
(Première dose): 11.340.554
<u>(Seconde dose): 3.977.046</u>

Le taux d'incidence (nombre de personnes infectées dans une région pour 100.000 habitants).
Le taux de reproduction du virus: **le R.**
Si vous êtes testé positif à la Covid, vous devez vous isoler pendant 10 jours.
Les cas contacts doivent s'isoler pour une durée de 7 jours.
Le taux de positivité (% des cas positifs sur le nombre de personnes testées).
La tension hospitalière (le niveau de saturation des services de réanimation).
Covid-19: les vrais chiffres de la réanimation: les personnes en soins critiques: 5 254 dont 3 963 personnes en réanimation (life-support) et 1 291 personnes en soins intensifs ou surveillance continue (4 avril 2021).
Le nombre de décès du coronavirus en France a dépassé la barre de 100.000 (mai 2021).

Les symptômes de la Covid-19/du coronavirus:
- la toux
- la fièvre
- la perte du goût ou de l'odorat
- le nez qui coule
- le mal de gorge

Il y a aussi des personnes infectées qui sont asymptomatiques.

Les mesures pour lutter contre la Covid et arrêter sa propagation:

> **Pratiquez/respectez les gestes barrières**
> **Le port d'un masque** est obligatoire (dans les magasins, les transports publics…).
> **La distanciation sociale** d'un ou deux mètres.
> **Toussons et éternuons dans le coude.**
> **Lavons-nous les mains** regulièrement.
> **Utilisons un mouchoir jetable.**

Le confinement (lockdown): fermeture des restaurants, des magasins non-essentiels, des coiffures, des cinémas, etc.; fermeture des écoles; fermeture des lieux de culte (places of worship); favoriser le télétravail; ne sortir que pour faire des achats ou pour faire de l'exercice ou pour promener le chien; limitez vos contacts/ne pas rencontrer des personnes d'autres ménages; l'interdiction de voyages non-essentiels.

Le couvre-feu (curfew) à partir de 18h jusqu' à 6h.

La fermeture des frontières.

La quarantaine pour ceux qui sont testés positifs au virus.

Les cas contacts doivent aussi s'isoler.

Tester/tracer/isoler
Le système de traçage est-il efficace?
Les centres de dépistage (test centres).
Le dépistage: des tests salivaires, des tests naropharyngés (rapid or lateral flow device (LFD) which are swab tests that give results in 30 minutes or less, without the need for processing in a laboratory), des tests PCR (polymerase chain reaction swab tests processed in a laboratory), des tests rapides anti-géniques, des auto-tests, des tests aléatoires (random tests).
Le séquençage des génomes pour indentifier des mutations (les variants britannique, sud-africain, brésilien et indien (rebaptisé Delta)).

Le programme de vaccination
Encourager toute la population à se faire vacciner: les personnes qui sont anti-vaccins, la crainte des effets secondaires (maux de tête, nausée, fatique, coagulation de sang...).
Les centres de vaccination/les vaccinodromes.
Les vaccins Pfizer/AstraZenica/Moderna/Johnson et Johnson, et le vaccin russe Spoutnik V.
La priorisation aux vaccinations:
- les résidents et les soignants dans les EHPAD;
- les médecins, les infirmiers et les soignants dans les hôpitaux;
- les patients avec comorbidités; les patients avec des pathologies graves devraient se faire vacciner le plus vite que possible.
Il est important d'accélérer les vaccinations: la production, la livraison et le déploiement.
L'EMA (L'Agence Européenne des Médicaments) autorise le stockage du vaccin Pfizer à des températures de congélateurs.
L'EMA constate un lien entre le vaccin AstraZenica et les rares cas de thrombose. Le bénéfice en faveur du vaccin reste incontestable.
Le bénéfice-risque des vaccins est largement favorable.
Est-il possible de rendre obligatoire la vaccination? (Par exemple, pour le personnel dans les EHPAD).

La gestion de la crise
Le succès des laboratoires et des fabricants de vaccins.
La protection des personnes âgées et les soignants dans les Ehpad.
La commande et le manque des vêtements sanitaires, des gants et des masques.
Les retards dans la commande et la livraison des vaccins; le manque de séringues et d'aiguilles.
L'homologation des vaccins par l'EMA et par les agences nationales.
L'efficacité des vaccins Pfizer et AstraZenica; l'efficacité du système de traçage.
Les mutations du virus: comment contrôler la propagation des mutations/les souches (strains) du virus/les variants anglais, sud-africain, brésilien et indien?
La protection des médecins et des infirmiers; éviter de saturer/engorger les hôpitaux; le report de traitements des patients avec d'autres pathologies.

Pour désengorger les services de réanimation dans les hôpitaux en Île-de-France, on transfère quelques patients dans d'autres régions qui sont sous moins de tensions hospitalières, par des TGV médicalisés et par hélicoptère.
Faire un tri/trier des patients n'est pas un bon terme, on fait de la *priorisation*.

Le déconfinement: relaxing lockdown measures **en étapes** *in stages*.

Éviter **un reconfinement:** avoid a **reimposition of lockdown.**

Une feuille de route (a way-bill) a road map/a plan:
La vaccination de toute la population.
Un passeport vaccinal/un pass(e) sanitaire.
Le contrôle et la quarantaine des passagers internationaux.
Retour des écoles et des universités: respect d'un protocole sanitaire strict; des tests salivaires réguliers.
Réduire la jauge dans les stades de sports.

Continuez à pratiquer/appliquer les gestes barrières.
Vacances à l'étranger: sont-elles possibles?
Réouverture progressive de l'économie.

L'impact sur l'économie
Des aides pour protéger des emplois; des aides pour ceux qui ont
perdu leurs emplois, leurs entreprises, leur moyen de gagner leur
vie, leur capacité de payer les factures, de se nourrir.
Les banques d'alimentation/les restaurants bénévoles; les *Restos
du Coeur* is a French charity, set up in 1985 on the initiative of
the comedian Coluche, to distribute food packages and hot meals
to those in need;
L'alimentation et des abris pour les sans-abris;
Les repas gratuits pour certains enfants pendant les vacances
scolaires.
Les finances publiques: faudra-t-il augmenter les impôts? Comment
combattre le chômage et l'inflation?

L'impact sur l'enseignement des jeunes: l'efficacité et les
problèmes des leçons à distance; l'évaluation via le contrôle continu
par les professeurs au lieu d'examens; cours de rattrapage …
L'impact sur la santé physique et mentale de ceux qui ont
été impactés: les jeunes et leur enseignement; ceux qui ont perdu
des proches; ceux qui ont été interdits de voir leur mère ou père
dans un Ehpad etc; ceux qui n'ont pas pu assister à des obsèques
etc. L'isolement (*loneliness*) des gens.
La forme longue de la Covid-19 ("Covid long"): de nombreux
patients souffrent encore de symptômes plusieurs mois après avoir
été malades de la Covid- 19: fatique extrême, difficulté à respirer,
pertes de mémoire… ce qui peut nécessiter une réadmission à
l'hôpital. Ces patients peuvent présenter *des séquelles* (consequential
medical complications/sequelae), notamment l'altération (impairing)
d'un ou plusieurs organes: les poumons (lungs), le coeur (heart),
les reins (kidneys), le foie (liver), l'intestin et le système nerveux.
Analyse des communautés les plus atteintes par le virus;
les personnes plus à risque; les conséquences des reports de

traitements pour des patients avec d'autres pathologies graves/ avec comorbidités.

Une augmentation de salaires pour nos médecins, infirmiers et soignants qui sont épuisés?
Une enquête sur l'efficacité des mesures prises et la compétence du gouvernement et le respect des mesures par nous tous?
Comment mieux nous protéger dans l'avenir contre de tels virus?
- Comment atteindre l'immunité collective contre la Covid-19?
- Peut-on mélanger les différents types de vaccins qui sont injectés?
- Est-ce qu'une troisième dose du vaccin/une dose de rappel (a "booster" jab) est nécessaire pour toute la population?
- Qu'est-ce qu'on peut mieux faire pour aider les vaccinations dans les pays moins favorisés?

Appendix 12
Clarification of French Covid Restrictions

> **MERCI DE**
>
> **PRÉSENTER VOTRE**
>
> **<u>PASS SANITAIRE</u>**
>
> **AU SERVEUR**

Clarification of French Covid Restrictions

Le gouvernement français tente d'éclaircir les mesures applicables
aux habitants dans les zones avec restrictions sanitaires renforcées:
16 départements (23 mars 2021);
19 départements (28 mars 2021);
Et sur tout le territore entre le 3 avril et le 2 mai 2021.

Dedans avec les miens

Je ne reçois pas chez moi;
Je ne me rends pas chez les autres;
Je télétravaille sauf impossibilité;
J'aère regulièrement mon logement;
Je ne sors plus après 19h.

Dehors en citoyen

Je porte le masque et je respecte les distances.
J'évite de manger ou de boire si je ne suis pas seul ou avec les
personnes de mon foyer.
Je ne quitte pas ma région ou mon département sauf motif impérieux
ou professionnel justifié par attestation.
Je peux sortir jusqu'à 19h pour des motifs autorisés:
* travailler;
* me promener;
* faire des courses;
* accompagner mes enfants à l'école;
* sortir mon animal de compagnie;
* aller chez le médecin.

Au-delà de 10 kilomètres, je dois avoir une attestation justifiant le motif de mon déplacement.

Je peux retrouver des amis dehors, mais à 6 maximum en respectant les gestes barrières.

Since 2 May 2021, these measures were progressively relaxed. *Le couvre-feu* (curfew) was extended to 23.00 hours (until 30th June 2021); a last-minute dispensation, however, was allowed for specatators at the epic late-evening Djokovic v Nadal semi-final match at Roland-Garros. As a result, there followed some non-authorised breaches of the rules. *La lassitude gagnait du terrain. Le non-respect des règles prenait de l'ampleur.*

On 16th June 2021, Jean Castex, the Prime minister, announced that:

- Le port du masque à l'extérieur n'est plus obligatoire, sauf dans un lieu bondé, une file d'attente, un marché ou au stade.
- Le couvre-feu sera levé le 20 juin (au lieu du 30 juin).

The official statistics showed that, at that time, new average daily Covid cases in metropolitan France were fewer than 5,000; and that the number of people in hospital was below 13,000 and continuing to fall, as was the number of intensive care cases (under 2000) and the number of daily deaths (around 60 or below). The above-mentioned relaxation of measures – in response to this downward trend in cases and deaths – coincided with the start of the summer season when circulation of the virus was expected to diminish. There was a fear that a fourth wave (*une quatrième vague*) of the virus might arrive in the autumn. The Delta / Indian variant was present in France but had so far not taken hold as it had in the UK. It was essential for a high proportion of the population to be double vaccinated as soon as possible.

With rising cases of the Delta variant in other countries, including Tunisia, and a worsening situation in the French overseas regions of La Réunion and Martinique, Emmanuel Macron made a televised address to the French nation on 12 July 2021. He announced *"un été de mobilisation"* in which he urged the whole population to get vaccinated.

He announced stringent vaccination measures:
- to make vaccination compulsory for all health workers, other non-care staff and volunteers working in hospitals, clinics and retirement homes; and also, for those workers (including fire and ambulance service personnel) coming into contact with elderly and vulnerable people. (Controls and sanctions would be imposed from 15th September 2021 for those not complying);
- to make it a requirement to possess and present *un pass sanitaire* (a Covid health certificate) to be able to attend cultural or leisure activities involving over 50 persons (from 21st July 2021); and in order to be able to enter public places such as cafés, restaurants, theatres, commercial centres and hospitals; and to take long distance travel by train, coach or plane (from 9th August 2021);
- a programme of vaccinations in secondary schools would specifically target school pupils (*collégiens et lycéens*) i.e., 12 years old and above, once the schools had returned (*après la rentrée*) after the summer holidays (*les grandes vacances scolaires*).

A law, giving legal effect to these measures, was adopted by the French parliament on 26th July 2021. The requirement to show a *pass sanitaire* for entry into public places would not apply to 12-17 year olds until 30th September 2021. To get the *pass sanitaire* you must have shown proof of having been fully vaccinated, or of having had a negative PCR test within 48 hours (subsequently extended to 72 hours), or of having recovered from the virus in the previous six months.

Jean Castex, *le Premier ministre*, hoped that the objective of vaccinating 50 million French people (including 12-17 year olds), with a first injection, could be achieved by the end of August. Since the beginning of the pandemic around 113,000 people had died in France from Covid at this time.

A (third) booster jab *(une troisième dose du vaccin contre la Covid-19/ une dose de rappel)* was recommended for persons over 65, for those with health problems and for all residents of care homes (*les Ehpad*) from September 2021.

The fourth wave (*la quatrième vague*) has not been as severe as was first expected, largely as a result of the high number of vaccinations;

and also of the requirement for a *pass sanitaire* and the continued application of the *gestes barrières*. But, as in the UK, cases are again rising in the rest of Europe, as the protection from the second dose of the vaccine wears off after approximately six months.

On 9th November, in a further televised address to the French nation, Emmanuel Macron said that Europe was facing a fifth wave (*une cinquième vague*) of coronavirus infections. For example, a daily record number of new cases had been recorded in Germany (over 50,000) and in the Netherlands (over 16,000). In France, over 12,000 new cases had been registered on one day, which was the highest number since the beginning of September. In France, 75% of the population had been fully vaccinated, with over 51 million people having received one dose of a vaccine, and over 50 million having received a second dose or completed their vaccine programme. President Macron urged all non-vaccinated persons (from the age of 12 years) to get vaccinated. He announced that all persons over 65 needed to get a (third) booster jab (*une dose de rappel*) by 15th December, as the validity of the health pass (*le pass sanitaire*) would not otherwise be extended to them. A booster jab would be available to all persons over 50 from the beginning of December.

The coronavirus data as at 18th November are:

Le tableau de bord (au 18 novembre 2021)
Nombre de nouveaux cas confirmés: 20.366
Nombre de personnes hospitalisées: 7.782
Nombre de patients en réanimation: 1.333
Décès (en 24h/total): 57/119.000
Nombre de vaccinations:
Première dose: 51.637.410
Seconde dose/schéma vaccinal complet: 50.559.570
Dose de rappel (troisième dose): 5.300.300

La France est en état d'alerte sur le plan sanitaire avec la recrudescence des nouveaux cas de la Covid-19, mais aucun reconfinement n'est prévu à l'heure actuelle (le 23 novembre 2021).

In December, a new variant, Omicron, was first detected in South Africa, and has now spread rapidly in the UK and France, and in the rest of the world. Le variant Omicron est beacoup plus contagieux, mais ses effets sont moins sévères, que le variant Delta. At the beginning of January 2022, over 200,000 new infections were recorded in a single day in France; and further restrictions are being applied, including the introduction of *un pass vaccinal* (vaccination pass). Over 53 million people have now received a first dose of the vaccine and over 35 million have received a third booster dose. Vaccinations have also been approved in France for 5-11 year olds, on a voluntary basis. 5 million French people have not been vaccinated. President Macron is quoted, controversially, in an interview for the daily newspaper, le Parisien, as saying: "J'ai très envie d'*emmerder* les non-vaccinés".

Appendix 13
Gros Mots (Some swear words)

NB. *The use of these words may shock and offend. Avoid using them in polite company. It is sufficient to be able to understand them.*

Baiser qqn = to fuck someone (*embrasser qqn, faire la bise à qqn* = to kiss someone; *les bises, les bisous, les baîsers* are kisses). **Baiser qqn does not mean to kiss someone:**
"*Permettez-moi de baiser votre femme!*" (Gerald Hoffnung).
Putain = a prostitute; but as an expletive *putain!* means damn! *merde!* or *merde alors!* shit! *putain de merde!* a double dose of shit!
Vladimir Putin in French is written and pronounced: Vladimir Poutine.
Une poufiasse is a woman of loose morals; a tart; *une horizontale* = *une prostituée.*
Vous êtes con: You are an idiot!
Connard! You bloody stupid idiot / man!

À bas les mains, connard: Take your hands off me, you jerk!
Connasse: You bloody stupid woman!
Va te faire foutre: Fuck off!
Enculé: Arsehole! Bastard!
Va te faire enculer: Bugger off!
Dégueuler: to puke (*vomir, avoir l'estomac au bout des lèvres:* to be sick).
C'est dégueulasse: it's enough to make you puke (*c'est dégoûtant, écoeurant* – it's disgusting).
Vous êtes dégueulasse: You are disgusting! You make me want to puke!
Espèce de cochon! Pig! *Espèce de con!* Idiot!
Je me suis fait engueuler: I got a bollocking/was reprimanded. *Il m'a engueulé(e)*: He gave me a right bollocking, told me off in no uncertain terms.
Elle va gueuler: she's going to kick up a stink/shout/bawl/complain.
Ta gueule! Ferme ta gueule! Shut your gob!

Tu déconnes! You are taking the piss! You are making fun of me!
Tu te fous de ma gueule! (As above but stronger).
Le zizi, la bite, le zob, la pine, la queue, la verge, some words for le pénis.
Le sexe, le chat, la chatte, some words for le vagin.
Les roberts, les nichons, les nénés, les amortisseurs (= shock absorbers) are all words for *les seins* (a woman's breasts).
Les couilles, les valseuses: balls, testicles.
Je m'en bats les couilles! You don't say! I don't give a damn !
Le bordel: brothel. *Quel bordel! C'est le bordel!* What a mess!
Il y a du monde au balcon refers to a woman with a full bosom/big tits.
Le cul: arse, backside.
Il veut le beurre et le prix du beurre et le cul de la crémière: (he wants the butter, the price of the butter, and he wants to make love to the milk maiden too).
[*Il veut le beurre et le prix du beurre*: He wants his cake and eat it – is <u>not vulgar</u>].
Un faux cul is someone who is two-faced.
Ne vous cassez pas le cul: Well don't bust a gut!
Je me casse le cul pour rien: I'm flogging a dead horse.
C'est chiant: It's annoying It's boring.
C'est emmerdant; vous êtes emmerdant (e), vous m'emmerdez: you are pissing me off.
Foutez-moi le camp! Clear off! *Foutez-moi la paix!*
On est foutus: We are fucked! We're doomed! We've had it!
(Un) salaud: bastard!
(Une) salope: trollop.
C'est vachement bien: It's bloody good!

Shakespeare & Company Book Shop, Latin Quarter, Paris

Bibliography

F.S. Pearson: Fractured French 1950
Pr. David Khayat: Arrêtez de vous priver 2021
Henriette Walter: Le français dans tous les sens 1986
Paris Match: Edition of 14 August 1981
Punch Magazine Special Issue: 24–30 March 1976
What French Connection?

Denys Parsons: Funny ha ha and funny peculiar 1965

Jim Hankinson: Bluff Your Way in Paris 1987

Gérard Roland: Stations de Métro 2011
E. & O. Bled: Cours supérieur d'orthographe 1969
Jean-Joseph Julaud:
Le français correct pour les Nuls 2004

L'Académie française:
Les rectifications de l'orthographe 1990

Harraps French-English Dictionary
Petit Larousse French Dictionary
Le Robert Dictionnaire des difficultés du français 2006
C News (French TV)

La Baie des Anges, Nice

Remerciements

I would like to thank everyone who has purchased a copy of this book.

Une Sortie de la Station de Métro Châtelet

Table of Contents

Le Château d'If, Marseille

Beaulieu–sur–Mer

Vallauris

Arles

Le Jas de Bouffon, Aix-en-Provence

Le Pont du Gard

La Maison Carrée, Nîmes

Le Mont-Saint-Michel

Auvers-sur-Oise

The author

Peter Voice attended Forest Boys' School in Horsham, West Sussex. He studied French and Economics at Kingston Polytechnic, including an academic year at the University of Rennes, Brittany. He subsequently worked for the Civil Service in London, and also lived and worked in Brussels for several years. More recently, he spent over 15 years as a tour manager, accompanying groups of American students and adults on cultural trips in the UK and continental Europe.

The illustrator Christian Gastaldello studied graphic design at Ealing School of Art and Design, and Art History at UCL. His extensive career in central government enabled him to travel to Europe, North America and to mainland China which has influenced his work, particularly in printmaking. He has participated in various London-based group shows.

The publisher

*He who stops
getting better
stops being good.*

This is the motto of novum publishing, and our focus
is on finding new manuscripts, publishing them and
offering long-term support to the authors.
Our publishing house was founded in 1997, and since
then it has become THE expert for new authors and
has won numerous awards.

**Our editorial team will peruse each manuscript
within a few weeks free of charge and without
obligation.**

You will find more information about
novum publishing and our books on the internet:

www.novum-publishing.co.uk